W9-BIZ-097

ALSO BY BILL KAUFFMAN

Every Man a King

Country Towns of New York

With Good Intentions?:
Reflections on the Myth of Progress in America

America First!
Its History, Culture, and Politics

Dispatches from the
Muckdog Gazette

To Nancy,
with all best wishes,
Bill Kpr
March 2003

Dispatches from the *Muckdog Gazette:*

A Mostly Affectionate Account of a Small Town's Fight to Survive

BILL KAUFFMAN

Henry Holt and Company | New York

Henry Holt and Company, LLC
Publishers since 1866
115 West 18th Street
New York, New York 10011

Henry Holt® is a registered trademark of
Henry Holt and Company, LLC.

Copyright © 2002 by Bill Kauffman
All rights reserved.

Library of Congress Cataloging-in-Publication Data
Kauffman, Bill, date.
Dispatches from the Muckdog Gazette : a mostly affectionate account
of a small town's fight to survive / Bill Kauffman.—1st. ed.
p.   cm.
ISBN 0-8050-6854-6 (hb)
1. Batavia (N.Y.)—Social life and customs.   2. City and town life—
New York (State)—Batavia.   3. Batavia (N.Y.)—Social conditions.
4. Kauffman, Bill, date.   5. Batavia (N.Y.)—Biography.   I. Title.

F129.B3 K38   2003
974.7'92—dc21   2002068943

Henry Holt books are available for special
promotions and premiums. For details contact:
Director, Special Markets.

First Edition 2003

Designed by Paula Russell Szafranski

Printed in the United States of America

10   9   8   7   6   5   4   3   2   1

To Michael,

my brother,

who is not related to Cleveland Elam

To its fugitive children, Grand Republic will forgive almost anything, if they will but come back home.

—SINCLAIR LEWIS, *CASS TIMBERLANE*

I think I'm goin' back. . . .

—DUSTY SPRINGFIELD

Contents

Dispatches from the *Muckdog Gazette*

Introduction

*S*o, what went wrong?"
  The small-town boy moving home from the City (any city, really: New York, Chicago, Boise, Walla Walla . . .) hears that question from every knew-he'd-never-make-it smirker he meets. After all, one does not *choose* repatriation to the provinces; the homecoming must be a sign of failure, a punishment, a public humiliation meted out for hubris. Home may be where the heart is, but the body is usually long gone. In the typical American success story, the heart is the only organ that *isn't* transplanted.

"If you were any good you'd be in the City."

Parents beam with pride as they tick off the residences of their college-educated children: often as not soulless hellholes such as Orlando and Myrtle Beach or the Wildewoode Lanes of transient suburbia. But parental pride wanes when someone brings up the names of those offspring who have not escaped the bounds of the old hometown.

Consider a pair of colloquialisms. "He'll go far," approving elders say of promising youngsters. This is consistent with the popular notion that success can be measured in terms of the distance one has traveled from home. If, on the other hand, we say of a boy, "He's not going anywhere," we are not praising him for his steadfast loyalty but damning him as an ambition-less sluggard.

Absence may make the heart grow fonder, but love's truest,

greatest expression, I have come to believe, is *im*mobility. Genuine fastness requires not locomotion but lack of motion.

Yet the mobile rule. Virtually every faxer and taxer in Washington, D.C., or on Wall Street has migrated for money or other manifestations of "the vain low strife that makes men mad," in William Cullen Bryant's phrase. (The good gray poet himself rode the social elevator from the pre-resort-defiled Berkshires to Manhattan.) It is beyond the ken of strivers why someone would not move when "opportunity" rears its meretricious head. Leaving home—forsaking home—is something every bright-eyed American child is expected to do, like hating her parents or whining about how nothing ever happens in this hick town of hers.

From Maine to Montana, "this hick town," source of national pith and myth, is disappearing into the Great American Nothingness. I want you to consider what is about to be lost.

This is a book about remaining in one place. About staying instead of straying. About not going anywhere—and being the richer for it.

I am—fanatically, unapologetically—a *placeist*. This makes me a virtual thought-criminal in an age of global homogeneity. "Placeism" might be defined in the criminal code as the unreasoned love of a particular place, be it a neighborhood, village, city, or even state. Placeists insist that residents of real places have histories, customs, accents, and concerns that are irreducibly different from those of other places. We believe that one town is not pretty much like the next, whatever the frequent flyer–mileage collectors of the NYC–LAX nexus might think. The differences between my Batavia, New York, and your town go well beyond the last names of the night-shift managers at Taco Bell and the Auto Zone.

I came home to Batavia (population 16,256 and shrinking by the decennial count) in 1988, accompanied by my skeptical but game Los Angeles–bred wife, Lucine. (It's Armenian for Darlene.) I had worked as a Senate staffer and editor in Washington and Southern California, happily surrounded by far more dear hearts and witty pals than competitive careerist assholes. But finally a vague suspicion that I had nursed since college concretized into a massive and unshakeable conviction: that a life lived anywhere but in my natal place would be fugitive, evanescent, meaningless. I had to go back.

So our friends Carlos and Troy helped us pack the U-Haul, and we were off on what I pledged would be a "one-year experiment" in coming home to a city which was then scrapping its venerable road-sign motto "Community of Opportunity" in favor of the less sanguine "Please Drive Carefully." The optimism of midcentury, when Batavia's factories hummed and Main Street bustled and the surrounding farms grew novelists and congressmen, had wilted like an orchid from the Wal-Mart Lawn and Garden Center.

Our year at home, as it turns out, has been of Old Testament duration. And if we have not supped nightly on milk and honey, neither have we been swarmed by a plague of locusts. However stumblingly, one native has returned.

I was not the first. I was hardly the most eminent. A rock star—not a Sirius, but no red dwarf either—preceded me. With dignity. While everything else in this book is flat-out fact, allow me to change a name or two in this Batavia parable.

Randy was Batavia's guitar virtuoso. Upon graduation from Batavia High he hooked up with a mid-'70s Upstate band that went by one of those names that brings shudders to the hip. Let's call it Kool Doodz. By that time I was into cerebral punk, so I scorned Randy's band in the way that a chess-club ectomorph deplores the brutality of football players.

A thousand and one reverberant nights in quarter-draft bars ignoring the drunks shouting "Skynyrd!" paid off. Kool Doodz signed on the dotted corporate line. They cut a record. They released a single. It crept into the Top 200. My brother Mike once played it several times consecutively on a jukebox in a Cleveland bar. Bringing the best of Batavia to benighted Buckeyes.

Randy's band filmed an early video that was played twice or thrice on MTV. Bound in an absurd red jumpsuit, he gamely disported with lip-licking models pretty enough to be featured in industrial clamp calendars. I think Randy even had a line in an *ABC Afterschool Special*: it must have contained the word "gig."

The Batavia *Daily News*, our newspaper of record, ran a feature on Randy. It bore a title like "Pizza Maker Hits the Big Time," for Randy had once worked in Batavia's oldest pizza shop, tossing pepperoni on the local delicacy. He was typically humble in this Hollywood dispatch, allowing that he was lucky to have hit the big time, and that Eddie Van Halen is a good guy once you get to know him. A framed copy of the article was hung on the pizza shop wall.

But all things, good and otherwise, must end. Even Kool Doodz. The band broke up. Artistic differences.

And so when I picked up my first pizza as a repatriated Batavian, who should be working the register but Randy—just a garlic exhalation or two away from the prominently displayed "Pizza Maker Hits the Big Time" clipping.

Would you like mushrooms on your mortification?

Randy's return struck me at first as a ghastly abasement. A hair shirt too prickly for even the most self-abnegating ascetic. But my embarrassment for him soon turned to admiration. He had guts. He knew his *place*—profoundly. He had a sense of security, a fixity, born of that knowledge. He was heroic. And when a year or so later I stealthily supplemented my meager income by working the midnight to 8 A.M. shift checking in groggy Winnebago-borne nomads at a local campground, I thought of Randy. Kool Doodz *rocks*, man.

Teachers and cops in those swatches of rural America that haven't been depopulated or defaced by military bases or Interstate exchanges speak of the comforting sense of familiarity that long years in one place can bring. Pretty girls beget pretty girls, just as the wild boys and their police-blotter antics are renewed with each generation.

The names and faces remain the same: only the hair lengths change. Life in such places seems less ephemeral, and it is. Things *stick*. My great-grandfather, long dead, looks over my shoulder. I struck out on the ball field of my father's glories. In Los Angeles I might be "here today, gone tomorrow," but in Batavia I will be one of you forever; it was in me before I was born and I will be of it after I die.

With shared memory and the mythicization of the everyday our lives take on layers of meaning. The alternative is existences lived on the edge of the abyss. We lose ourselves in crowds, yet a terrible fear of anonymity haunts many Americans: we want to be known, remembered, thought of, and except in the tawdriest sense this is only possible in small communities and networks of families. Those cut off from such possibilities are driven to freakish acts of exposure, such as flashing strangers on blue cable channels or running for president.

My maternal grandmother, Mary Stella Baker, eighty-eight, still drives the two-lane roads of Genesee County four nights a week to play Bingo at the town fire halls. She mutters "you sonofabitch" toward whichever lardass wins the jackpot. She has favorite and least-favorite numbers ("damn you, B-10") and when I accompany her she watches my single card in addition to her six boards. Grandma hand-grinds the Thanksgiving stuffing every November; she greets my father's hints of "Pepperidge Farm" with a hiss usually reserved for early Bingoers.

With almost the same frequency as she plays Bingo, Grandma Baker visits the funeral parlor, where she says good-bye to friends she has known since the days when she picked dandelions for tran-substantiation into wine in her parents' speakeasy. I hope one day to do the same. (I also plan to outlive my friends.)

Grandma was born, bred, and has lived all her life in the neigh-boring town of Le Roy. She is Italian: a "black dago," as Irish hellions once called her, though Grandma is quick to point out that she is "Northern Italian—almost Swiss."

Her parents warned her against taking up with the "stompers"—Sicilians purpling their feet with smushed grapes. So Grandma married a Baptist, but her sister Anna married Johnny, a man of the wine-dark Mediterranean. For decades the beloved Uncle Johnny has kept family oenophiles stocked with his homemade "dago red."

I realize that I am treading on sensitive ground here. We live in an age in which ethnic differences are not subject for discussion or—God forbid—humor. Instead, we are ordered to "celebrate our diversity," which in practice means extracting every white-ethnic spice and tang until gruel is all that simmers in the American melting pot. As for me and Batavia—give us the dagos any day.

Like all true-born daughters of Genesee County, Grandma and Anna are acutely aware of national origins. For instance, they identify Poles by their plateau-like noggins. Upon spotting a suspected son or daughter of Kosciusko, one sister will nudge the other and whisper, "Flathead."

Grandma and Anna laugh like teenage girls. They belong to their town, and it to them—every flathead and wop and Irishman. Before the Interstate ramp dumped an SUV-load of yuppies into picturesque Le Roy, everyone in town had a nickname. Reindeer. Chink. Eggs Bacon. Nig. (Surprisingly, "Nig" was a swarthy Irishman. When Nig died at home, his five-year-old grandson entered local folklore by appearing on the porch and gravely announcing to vigil-keeping relatives, "He's as dead as a doornail.")

Grandma carries on this dying tradition, even nicknaming the infants baby-sat by my cousin's wife. My favorite is "Little Alfred," who had an unfortunate resemblance to the director Hitchcock.

In March 1996, Grandma, Aunt Anna, and Uncle Johnny stood in my parents' backyard, sharing the early spring chill with a passel of Kauffmans. We were looking for Comet Hyakutake.

I am an astronomy buff from way back, ever since a Polish prince of a man welded a tripod for my little 3-inch telescope. But I had never seen a comet. When Halley's made its smudgy return in 1986,

I was encamped in Southern California, where the man-made light so besmears the sky that only the falsest stars can be glimpsed.

We resolved Hyakutake through my new binoculars, a gift from Jane, the aunt who forbade us to call her "Aunt." Jane is smart, pretty, devoted to her nephews, and stylish. This last trait proved untransmissible. When my brother and I were boys she'd buy us Van Heusen shirts with collars of a different color than the sleeves; one might just as well have entered Batavia Junior High wearing a sign-board reading "Please Beat the Shit Out of Me." When I published my only novel in 1989, Jane encouraged the family to take "coping lessons" to deal with my inevitable fame: a charming case of auntly optimism of which I hope she is never cured.

Quite undaunted by my fame, the comet-seekers stepped from the Kauffman backyard into Al McNabb's garden for a better view. Al McNabb was ninety-seven at Hyakutake's arrival. He remembered Comet Halley. As long as I could remember, from dawn to dusk, from spring to fall, this retired director of the YMCA hoed and planted and pulled weeds and told the occasional joke about his ancestry. (How was the Grand Canyon dug? A Scotsman dropped a dime.) The previous summer, Al, leaning on a rake, his face drenched in sweat, had squinted at me and said, "I'm getting awfully old for this, Billy."

"Ah, Mr. McNabb, you'll be out here forever," I replied with my usual obtuseness. But when Hyakutake bid us farewell in the spring of 1996, so did Al McNabb.

In his spare time, Mr. McNabb had helped launch the career of Barber Conable, our longtime congressman and the best that Republicans (or Democrats) are liable to produce in the statesman line. Conable would eulogize the Y director at his Methodist funeral service.

Al's wife, Ola McNabb, whose rhubarb-strawberry pie recipe keeps me sated every merry month of May, was the Republican election worker at our polling place—coincidentally the YMCA. Those voting at the Y first had to shake hands with Reverend Harold Milward, the Methodist minister who dressed up as Uncle Sam every

Election Day. However radical my politics have been, the impulse to revolution is always snuffed by the memory of Reverend Milward strolling the Y in his Uncle Sam beard and star-banded tall hat. Overthrow *that*? I think not.

I still recall Mrs. McNabb's crest falling when I voted for the first time and she could not find my name in the thick stack of GOP registrants. Only the dagos and flatheads and union men were Democrats in Batavia: surely I was not one of *them*! I lowered my head, apologetically, and disappeared behind the voting-machine curtain to pull the lever for her friend Barber Conable.

From the McNabb garden, Comet Hyakutake was brilliant in its last appearance before disappearing into moonglow. It etched the western sky just over the haze of the lights from Batavia Downs. The Downs, the oldest nighttime harness-racing track in the country, is where next month's hamburgers canter until they are buried. In a variation on the traditional dog and pony show, the horses combine with the Muckdogs, our minor league baseball team, to give Batavia its sporting reputation. (My late Grandpa Kauffman was an habitué of the track, penciling each night's programs with equine hieroglyphics and then betting on the horse with the catchiest name.) McNabbs, Kauffmans, Randys, Muckdogs: we are the ones who bet on Batavia. You can call us suckers; I think we're romantics. Our nag is a long shot, hard-ridden and sometimes ill-used, but she's still gimping around the track.

As we breathed in the cold night air, Grandma and Aunt Anna spoke of seeing a comet in their girlhood. Their family—the Stellas— had watched it from the front porch. "Cometa Stellata," they called it. The family comet. I thereby claimed Hyakutake as our comet.

Perhaps someday my daughter, Gretel, will tell her grandchildren about standing in the backyard of Grandma and Grandpa's house with her relatives, too soon gone, straining to glimpse something in the heavens. Is it too much to ask that she might someday stand in that same backyard? In a Batavia filled with the eccentric old ladies and Republican painters and holy farm-fed fools and saints and sinners (deserving of a million absolutions!) who animate my Batavia?

I once told a local audience, with a flattery bordering on fellatory, that the luckiest among us were those who never had left, the stationary set, unmoved by wanderlust or curiosity or the plain old shaking off of responsibility. Maybe. But in my truthful moods I remember the shock of pleasure when first I realized that the bright and well-bred twenty-two-year-old girls of Capitol Hill and Georgetown and DuPont Circle actually laughed at my jokes, took seriously my theories (which were less crackpot in those days: I was so much older then . . .), pulled me out on the dance floor, and even consented to actual dates. REO Speedwagon, Italians in Camaros, an informal if rigidly observed ban on polysyllabic words: Batavia was worlds away. I could blast Graham Parker from my secondhand record player or sit cross-legged in the grass reading Jones Very or write poems about baseball and pumpkins without arousing suspicions of faggotry or post-adolescent cooties. If I eventually came home a Confident Young Man, I owe it to the cosmopolitans. Which in my populist fury and sentimental wistfulness I must never forget.

Okay, I forgot.

What I remember, though, could fill a book . . .

CHAPTER ONE

Back to Batavia

I n John Gardner's novel *The Sunlight Dialogues*, a bearded wild man is arrested for painting "Love" in the middle of Oak Street in the sleepy western New York city of Batavia. He is jailed; he escapes; he is gunned down. The disturber of the peace is revealed to be Taggert Hodge, a local boy gone loco, a wandering son who returned to clue Batavians in to the mysteries of existence.

Poor Tag: he was a century and a half too late.

❏ ❏ ❏

One hundred and fifty years ago my native region of west-central New York blazed with the white fires of reform and fanaticism. Joseph Smith and Susan B. Anthony and Liberty Party abolitionists and a thousand ragged prophets traveled our "psychic highway," as folklorist Carl Carmer dubbed the Utica-to-Batavia corridor. We had Anti-Masons, reincarnated Christs, and enough necromancers to pester the dead till time's end.

The fires have long since dimmed in our region, which historians call the Burned-Over District. The scorched earth eventually grew verdant. Itinerant preachers became vagrants, and emancipationists took up temperance, vegetarianism, and other nuisance causes. Nothing flamed here anymore. So when I returned home in 1988, less hirsute than Taggert Hodge but no less feverish, I brought my own tinderbox.

I was going to be a one-man regionalist revival: a resuscitator of a weary, sluggish, beaten lump of a culture. To raise the dead and wake the living—to introduce them, to mate them, and watch a flowering of provincial genius the likes of which had never been seen before—this was my immodest aim.

Such grand visions clouded my eyes! I saw Grant Wood painting murals for Cedar Rapids businessmen. I saw Sinclair Lewis (whom a friend dubbed an "all-out professional Minnesotan") memorizing the Gopher State's eighty-seven counties and seats, just like his fictive Judge Cass Timberlane. I saw Sarah Orne Jewett greeting an awed little Mary Ellen Chase in South Berwick, kindly enjoining the girl to grow up and write stories "all about Maine." I saw Helen Hooven Santmyer, a mere factotum at the Dayton Library by day, smiling all the night as she wrote *Ohio Town* in celebration of her fair Xenia. I saw Hamlin Garland, the barefoot Dakota realist, having a man-to-man with William Dean Howells, and for an instant haughty Boston bowed before these two great midwestern writers. I saw Missouri's muscular artist Tom Benton on a Kansas City barstool and James Whitcomb Riley teaching America to speak Hoosier. I even saw Tennessee novelist Andrew Lytle walking on water where the TVA flooded his family's plantation. And I saw Upstate New York alive, again.

If you have an eagle eye, you can see the faint impress of a literary tradition in my New York. There were Cooper and Paulding and Irving, of course, although the latter two belonged to the Hudson Valley, which is too rich for our blood. Harold Frederic of Utica wrote some jarringly honest stories about Yorker ambivalence toward the Civil War. *The Damnation of Theron Ware*, his novel of a simple Upstate minister's faith-shattering encounter with the Enlightenment, is still assigned by American lit professors whose corpora are not yet occupied by race-gender pod people. (F. Scott Fitzgerald and Sinclair Lewis regarded it as among the finest of novels, period.)

In the dark years of the American midcentury our torch was carried by Walter D. Edmonds. His best-known historical novel, *Drums Along the Mohawk*, was kept from the top spot on the best-seller list of 1936 only by the contemporaneous release of some windy fiction about goings-on down South. (I knew Edmonds, who died in 1998 at the age of ninety-four. He was a courtly Harvard man whose ancestors included the Alcotts, yet the plain folk of his novels are far removed from fey Transcendentalists and earnest reformers. Edmund Wilson, the grumpy sage of nearby Talcottville, once told Edmonds to his face that he found his books "terribly dull" but did think him unequaled in writing about animals. Uh, thanks, Mr. Wilson.)

John Gardner set *The Sunlight Dialogues* and *The Resurrection* in Batavia. Frederick Exley did his boozy autobiographical thing in his gelid refuge Watertown. William Kennedy literarily owns Albany, that grafting outpost of empire, which is to Upstate as Guantanamo is to Cuba. My late friend Henry W. Clune, once America's oldest living novelist (he died at 105), wrote well about Rochester. Warren Hunting Smith committed Episcopalian Geneva to paper. Sheep farmer Ann Mohin crafted *The Farm She Was*, one of the finest first novels of recent years. That mountain in the distance, sometimes ours and sometimes not, is of course Edmund Wilson, Tory anarchist. See him inhaling vodka, studying the Iroquois, measuring his family tree, yelling at those goddam kids racing motorcyles on the street where he lived.

Wilson is, to put it gently, problematic for a western New Yorker. In the marvelously cranky *Upstate*, he complained that people west of Syracuse "seemed very low grade. Not even pretty girls, but pale gray-eyed lean ill-built Polish women and the usual thick loutish men. One wonders how these men and women can feel enough mutual attraction even to breed more of their unattractive kind." Et tu, Bunny?

And then, standing on the shoulders of these giants, tracing in their pencil grooves, came me. My first novel, *Every Man a King*, was published in 1989. (I can report that its tenth anniversary came and went with nary a Festschrift.) The book was about a young smart-aleck who works for a senator in Washington, D.C. He sins—at least as sin is defined in the Potomac catechism—and is cast out, home-ward, to live among The People. His People. Who annoy him to no end by refusing to act like Tom, Ma, and the rest of the noble Joads.

Not to spoil the ending for the handful of folks who have never devoured this classic, but the revenant returns for good. Because I, too, had taken the down-bound train to D.C. and back, folks seemed to think the novel was autobiographical. It was not. But just as John P. Marquand learned the hard way that "before you name a character, look him up in the phone book," so did I learn a valuable lesson: never make your protagonist sexually maladroit. You will get nothing but pitying stares from friends and tears of mortification from your mother.

Like my doughtily dysfunctional hero, I did go home, for good. There I would eventually learn that healthy, life-giving parochialism exists in even the most dispirited and quotidian places—like my Batavia. In '88, I was on the verge of an imagined fame that is the ignis fatuus of all about-to-be-published writers. But though my novel masquer-aded as an assault on Washington, D.C.'s ideologue class, it con-tained (horrors!) a *message*: go home, young man. Return to Anniston, to Fargo, to Batavia, to Saginaw. Rediscover the permanent things; fight your battles under the parochial flag. Sinclair Lewis wanted (in all seriousness) Duluth to be the Athens of America; I would settle for making my postage stamp of ground no less. I wanted to be the nativest son.

So I came home, to Batavia, in Genesee County, where my ances-tors settled early, for Americans at any rate. My German forebears had arrived in the 1850s, the Irish in the 1880s, Italians in the 1900s, and English in the dim mists of time. They farmed, repaired Model T's, and supervised the construction of the Batavia watertower.

Grandpa Kauffman even ran for city council as a representative of the German-Irish Democracy. He lost.

Batavia had suffered more than most small cities in the dislocating years since the Second World War. Its glory days were in the distant past, in the Jacksonian era, when an itinerant gadfly named Captain William Morgan wrote a book exposing the rituals of Freemasonry. Morgan was kidnapped for his perfidy by local Masons. Presumed drowned, he was never seen again. An Anti-Masonic Party sprang up overnight. By 1828, Upstate New York was ablaze, and for five head-spinning years Batavia was capital of the American political fringe, an antebellum Waco. (For years Ev Norris, a family friend, headed Batavia's Masonic Lodge, which is akin to being the Rotary Club president of Sauk Centre.)

The Gilded Age was good to Batavia. Dean Richmond, president of the New York Central Railroad before the Vanderbilts stole it, lived a grandee's life on leafy East Main Street. The tracks he laid brought industries of all sorts—gun works, a plow company, manufactories of agricultural implements—to our town. Richmond, the Democratic party chairman of New York in the early 1860s, was instrumental in securing the presidential nominations of Stephen Douglas in 1860 and the honorably blood-shy warrior George McClellan in 1864. But Batavia was solidly for Lincoln, and has been Republican ever since. A blue-collar enclave surrounded by fertile black muck with its rows of onions and potatoes and corn, Batavia was a friendly little city, like one of Vachel Lindsay's prairie towns, but with more ethnic spice: the English and the Scots and the Germans coexisted uneasily with the Irish, and at century's dawn came a polyglot influx of Poles and Italians.

But progress came and washed my town away. In the heady morn of the postwar world, Kitty Carlisle's boytoy, Governor Thomas E. Dewey (the pride of Owosso, Michigan, but resident of New York City or its overspill, as our governors always are), determined to build his own Erie Canal, and the New York State Thruway was born.

Eminent domain came to rural York with a vengeance. Hundreds of miles of farmland were stolen by Albany, for the greater good, of course. This state-of-the-art roadway would link us with New York City, 400 short miles away. Think of the benefits!

The curmudgeons carped and the mossbacks muttered, as curmudgeons and mossbacks will do. Some mad farmers, sap of 1776 running within, took potshots at surveyors. But the Thruway was built. Its first casualty was Route 5, our Main Street, for years a bustling thoroughfare. Travelers ate at diners along Route 5—Critics, the Dagwood, Don's Dinette—and slept in motels, and shopped at stores (Carr's and Friedley's and Salway's). Then progress came, and the farms were paved, and Route 5 died. Across Upstate, countless locally owned and owner-operated businesses were bankrupted. Drivers stuck to the Thruway and ate the tasteless chain fare.

Batavia responded to the demise of Route 5 with an act of parricide unequaled this side of Romania, where the vampiric Ceauçescu once waged war on pre-Communist architecture. Our city fathers rushed headlong into urban renewal, whereby the federal government paid Batavia to knock down its past: the mansions of the founders, sandstone churches, the brick shops, all of it—even Dean Richmond's mansion, which had become an orphanage financed by Edna Gruber, the city's legendary madam with a heart of gold, may she rest in peace.

Batavia tore out—literally—its five-block heart and filled the cavity with a ghastly mall, a dull gray sprawling oasis in a desert of unused parking spaces. The mall was a colossal failure. Built in the aptly named Brutalist style, it is used in urban-planning texts as a case study in disaster. But it succeeded in destroying the last vestiges of our home-run economy. J. C. Penney and Wendy's were in; the Dipson Theater and the Dagwood were out. As the Chamber of Commerce might put it in one of those newspeak brochures, Batavia had entered the global economy.

Why did our town rip out its heart? Ask George Babbitt. Batavia's civic class has the same lust for progress that warped Sinclair Lewis's

Zenith. It is extraordinary to read through copies of the Batavia *Daily News* as the city was being leveled. Every few weeks another bank, hotel, tavern, or even church is blown up or torn down, and the razing is the subject of a gee-whiz photo on page one. But where is the outrage? In the paper's pages, the occasional merchant complains that he is being shortchanged, not getting enough from what amounts to an eminent domain fund. Yet apart from the Landmark Society, citizen criticism of the destruction is rare. For this was Progress, the almighty god of the Greatest Generation, in the phrase of Tom Brokaw's ghostwriter.

Progress was the idol of the cohort that gave us urban renewal and IBM and regarded long hair and pot smoking and Jefferson Airplane as sinful but sending your sons halfway around the globe to die for Robert McNamara as a supreme act of patriotism. It was the whole Baal-game of the generation that gulped down every last ounce of whatever snake oil was on sale, as long as it promised Profit and a More Abundant Future.

Batavia being Batavia, we were about five years behind the curve. Martin Anderson had published *The Federal Bulldozer*, his utter demolition of urban renewal, in 1964, when so much of our city might yet have been saved. Like the Babbitt bunch, Batavia craved "modern ideals." In 1976, as the mall squatted brutally over what once was, the *Daily News* fatuously editorialized that the naysayers "had to admit that Batavia accomplished a great deal."

The urban renewal officials all had un-Batavian names, and their progeny do not have to live with the ruin. From a distance of forty years, I take an especial scunner to one Walter D. Webdale, a young planner from Buffalo—that "self-important Buffalo," an "ant-hill so absurd" as Vachel Lindsay versified.

In 1963, when he was in his mid-twenties, Webdale became Batavia's director of urban renewal; he departed our ruined village in 1966 to urbanly renew Glen Cove, Long Island. Commissar Webdale spoke fluent Soviet: "[T]he arguments that the projects are not correctly designed, that there is too much use of the bulldozer . . . should be examined in light of their source and then discounted, to keep the program going." The Program Über Alles!

In response to an open letter from the Landmark Society asking the Urban Renewal Agency to "preserve the historic and aesthetic heritage" of Batavia, Webdale sneered that the city's built landscape had nothing "uniquely Batavian. We have things typically American from all over this part of the country." Nothing "uniquely Batavian"? As if the stone quarried, the wood hewn, the bricks laid, the tears and kisses and lives passed within the hundreds of homes and small shops on Webdale's hit list were abstract nothings.

Forgive them, Lord—though they knew very well what they were doing.

Progress was not the sole reason why Batavia obliterated the handiwork of her fathers. Also fueling the consuming blaze were class and ethnic resentments, which we are not allowed to talk about in Batavia under penalty of banishment. (Fortunately, my wife and I have moved five miles up Route 98 to the village of Elba, so the threat of exile is moot. I am already in Napoleonic isolation.)

Batavia's immigrants, particularly the Italians and Catholics, prospered in the middle years of our century. They surpassed the English and German natives—including the booboisie, which had barred them from country clubs and the like—and they came to feel, understandably, that Batavia needed a facelift to reflect its reconfigured ethnic mix. New, sometimes gaudy homes were built on the city's east end, branching out from the ominously named Naramore Drive. (The city's first jejune street name, this faux Indian tag hinted of suburban developments in hour-away Rochester, of Blueberry Hills without blueberries and Olde Westchester Drives that one could not survive without intravenous Rye.)

The old, dilapidating Greek Revival and Federal-style homes of the prosperous nineteenth-century Main Street burghers were deemed eyesores, paint-peeling relics of pre–Ellis Island days. As an elderly member of the displaced gentry observed, "It was just a hatred of the people who built Batavia."

Then again, the feckless sons and daughters of the people who built Batavia *deserved* a share of hatred. They abandoned the city, or let the Progress boys knock it down. Behind closed Presbyterian doors they derided the Italians as greasy vulgarians, but the Eyeties, to their everlasting credit, have been on the right side of virtually every political issue in Batavia in my lifetime, and even before. They have also been slower to discard ethnic appurtenances in the gradual fade into the Great American Nothingness.

At all events, it all came down, and the new Batavia looked like Dresden. When urban renewal was completed, it looked like Dresden with a grotesque mall sprouting from the rubble. Now, in a twisted way, it all makes sense. You see, suicide is my city's leitmotif. The two most famous Batavians of the nineteenth century, Holland Land Company agent Joseph Ellicott and post–Civil War military strategist and West Point Commandant Emory Upton, killed themselves. Ellicott hanged himself with his handkerchief in a New York City insane asylum, and Upton blew his brains out at the Presidio. But still, a *municipal* suicide? Surely no sane body politic could commit such madness.

Batavia did. Oh, there was grumbling about urban renewal among the working class and from some of the older families. Our friend Marge Gilhooly's aunt, Lucy Gilhooly, famous for wearing a cherry-filled hat emblazoned "Life Is a Bowl of Cherries," sat on the porch of the Trumbull Cary Mansion the morning it was to be destroyed. The Cary Mansion, built in 1817, had been given to the city in 1934 by a Cary descendant. The family had deserted Batavia, of course, but had hoped with a kind of charming vanity that their ancestral manse might become the Genesee County version of Mount Vernon. Alas, Trumbull wasn't even the father of his county, let alone his country, so down came his home, with a wrecking ball paid for by the federal government under the Hill-Burton Act. Technically, the

Catholics dunnit. The Sisters of Mercy, the order of nuns who ran St. Jerome Hospital, knocked down the Cary Mansion to make way for the architectural splendor of the McAuley School of Nursing. The Sisters, in turn, would be run out of town in an anti-Catholic pogrom in 1999, or about forty years too late.

Lucy Gilhooly, mad as a fruity hatter, fought the eccentric fight on the porch, but resistance was futile. The Greatest Generation was at the helm! And besides, in the late 1950s, Batavia had shifted from an elected mayor to the impeccably progressive city manager system, removing city administration from the messy muck of *politics* and, not incidentally, depriving us of the inevitable Italian and Polish mayors.

Every single city manager has been a credentialed outsider, tied to Batavia by nothing more substantial than paragraph three of a xeroxed resume. The demon seed of urban renewal spurted to life in a city planning board that was a spawn of the city manager system. And lethewards we went.

The destruction of old Batavia led to a housing shortage. Our poorest residents had for years lived above the small Main Street shops, in the respectable brick buildings of the late nineteenth century. They were in the *middle of things*, as Jane Jacobs and the later New Urbanists would say. But progress kicked them out on the streets. So Batavia, prodded by her concerned clergy and laity— including, incredibly to me, the imperious Monsignor Francis Schwartz, of whom more anon—secured federal monies to construct several typically ugly and depressing clusters of low-income housing, far away from Main Street.

As always, the pox was placed on working-class neighborhoods. Alas, or perhaps happily, we hadn't enough poor people to fill these jerry-built tenements. So Buffalo families, some of them black, were shipped in. Suddenly, Batavia had its first taste of race hatred.

Theretofore, a very small black community had existed in Genesee County. The Underground Railroad ran through our towns of Le Roy and Elba, although most of our black citizens had come up from the South in the great Dixie diaspora of the Second World War. Relations between the races had been classically Northern, distantly cordial if not close. The fallout from urban renewal changed that. The newcomers from Buffalo soon dominated the police blotter. The crimes were for the most part petty, but the animosities were real. "Lotta niggers in Batavia" became a common refrain, and pious exhortations to brotherhood and school celebrations of Martin Luther King Day changed nothing.

John Gardner thought his hometown had become emblematic of Main Street, U.S.A.'s decline:

> Batavia, New York . . . was, in the beginning, a wonderful, beautiful place with the smartest Indians in America around. Now it's this old, run-down town which has been urban-renewalized just about out of existence. The factories have stopped and the people are poor and sometimes crabby; the elm trees are all dead, and so are the oaks and maples. So it's a good symbol.

□ □ □

Silly me, full of pride and vainglory and the defiant spirit of my forefathers. I was to be the avenging ghost of old Batavia! I wanted to pour gasoline in one glorious wide path from Utica to Buffalo. Once ignited, the Burned-Over District would positively glow with fire, a beautiful consuming conflagration, and out of the flames a new Upstate would emerge, dreamy and boisterous and refractory, just like one hundred and fifty years ago.

Boy, was I ever stupid.

For one thing, I didn't listen to my Los Angelena wife. Lucine likes the landscape and appreciates the intimacy of lives lived locally, as opposed to lives sunbathed away in the Raybanned anonymity of her cradle. She is in fact on her way to becoming the new grande dame of Genesee County, but in her moments of cynical clarity Lucine scoffs that my Upstate, with its gallery of horse-sense philosophers and trailer park angels and adamantine Presbyterian dowagers, is somewhere between a mirage and a lie.

I didn't even listen to my novel, in which the chronically misfiring protagonist who bears no resemblance to the author is forced to confront the pitiless reality that Batavia's dirty blondes in halter tops have never heard of Edmund Wilson.

Perhaps mine is the commonest tale of the exile returning home. It begins with the longings of Booth Tarkington's *Gentleman from Indiana*: "The thought of coming back to a life-work in my native state appealed to me. I always had a dim sort of feeling that the people out in these parts knew more—had more sense and were less artificial."

I had spent several pleasurable years in Babylon—Washington, D.C., and Southern California, to be precise—until the usual pangs of homesickness grew into something quite different: a conviction that only by living in the place of my nativity, and the nativity of my ancestors, could I live a life that was anything but footloose and ephemeral. I still believe this, and always will. (As my fellow Upstater Frederick Exley said, "Watertown is not in my marrow; it is my marrow.")

When I take midnight walks, I feel the presence of ghosts. I pass an abandoned brick gashouse built by my great-grandfather Will Garraghan, a mason of the nonconspiratorial sort. I wander by the shut-down factory where my grandfather Ed Kauffman was shop steward. Thanks to great-great-uncle Dan Kauffman's supervisory genius (or so I like to think) the watertower has not collapsed. And almost daily I stroll the sylvan campus of the New York State School for the Blind, where grandmother Loretta Garraghan Kauffman taught Braille in the days before mainstreaming. One block from the family homestead is Dwyer Stadium, home of the Class-A Batavia Muckdogs, Bunyanesque heroes of generations of local kids. My dad was batboy, and for a few games I was, too; *Field of Dreams* syrup aside, and asking pardon for blasphemy, my every visit to Dwyer is an act of communion.

Coming home exerts especial appeal to the contrarians among us. Every economic, cultural, and societal pressure pushes us into the cities and their suburban spill, the bigger the better. Wendell Berry, an exemplary repatriated countryman, described this urbanizing force in *Remembering*:

> Years ago, he resigned himself to living in cities. That was what his education was for, as his teachers all assumed and he believed. Its purpose was to get him away from home, out of the country, to someplace where he could live up to his abilities. He needed an education, and the purpose of an education was to take him away.

Returning becomes an act of rebellion. But just as no one sings louder than the whore in church, no regional patriotism can match that of the returning prodigal. Through travel he has discovered what is unique about his homeplace; he insists on shouting these newfound truths from the rooftops—and boring his neighbors blue.

Southerners know this better than anyone. Proving Lord Acton's aphorism that exile is the nursery of nationalism, almost every one of the agrarian authors of the 1930 Southern manifesto *I'll Take My Stand* spent his early adulthood north of Mason-Dixon; Stark Young and Robert Penn Warren, among others, never returned. But they *did* look back, and that made all the difference. They had to see the City to love the Country.

Alas, localism is neater in theory than in practice.

I visited the mall on my first day home to draw the bead on my enemy. To my surprise, I could summon none of the old bile; all I felt was pity. No one was ever there.

The shops were deserted; fudgsicle-smeared urchins loitered around video games; fat women and vaguely remembered white trash classmates slumped on the L-shaped orange couches in the atrium.

A dozen years later, despite desultory talk about "tearing it down," nothing has changed. Except the urchins are blacker.

Just inside the western entrance a mural spanned the wall. High school students had painted—from pictures—what Main Street used to look like. Chuck's Sporting Goods, Scott & Bean, the Charles Men Shop: the colors were vivid, the effect somber. It's as if an unrepentant murderer were showing off his prize possession, a Polaroid of his hapless victim. See how pretty Nicole Simpson was?

Everywhere in Batavia I found small independent businesses in retreat. The Dutch-owned Tops grocery chain had opened a "superstore" on West Main Street, on the site of the Batavia arsenal to which patriots rallied after Buffalo was burned in 1813. All those little corner grocers, where three o'clock liberated-from-school kids bought pretzel sticks and Bazooka Joes and red hot dollars, all those Lambert's and Wandryk's and Say's and Borrelli's, are gone gone gone. (One corner store endures in its shabby magnificence, despite that nasty business about illegally trading in food stamps. You do what you gotta do.) The Tops superstore also has a pizza oven and even a gas pump, and a Domino's opened near Naramore, so Pontillo's and Matty's and Ficarella's and Uncle Tony's had better dig in and fight. Or maybe it would be easier to sell out, pack the wife and kids into a U-Haul, and slink ass down to Florida. To a trailer park reservation, with all the other white Indians.

Forsake family and faith for a few extra degrees Fahrenheit in Florida. Fuckers! Florida, the state so packed with trash that its richest man is garbage-industry king Wayne Huzienga. Trashy Wayne's repellent Blockbuster Video has invaded Batavia, squatting between Tops and Kmart. It has only one competitor in the city: Arena's, formerly a car dealership cum strip joint. (Only mammaries were uncovered, and only until neighborhood complaints shut it down.) I delight to spelunk in Nancy Arena's dank and phoneless store, with its un-Blockbusterish cache of '70s movies. You can have your life-size (if never lifelike) Jennifer Aniston and Keanu Reeves; Arena's is the only video store in America with special sections devoted to Gary Busey and Jan-Michael Vincent. Nancy charges one dollar less than Blockbuster for both old and new movies, yet the sheep insist on being fleeced by the chain.

The estimable Batavia *Daily News* has passed from the Griswolds and the McWains—stolid old Republicans, how gentle that Main Street Harding hauteur I once loathed now seems in the fog of retrospect—to a chain. Hardworking kids just out of college learn the trade at the *Daily News*, and do a more than creditable job, but absentee owners (the Johnson Newspapers of Watertown, which once refused to hire Fred Exley to write a column) are not the sort to undertake campaigns to save the county courthouse. (Ours lacked handicapped access, air conditioning, and day-care facilities.) Or keep out the Republicans' favorite jobs program—new prisons. One of Batavia's biggest employers is the new Immigration and Naturalization Service holding center, a.k.a. The Prison, which our former congressman, the callow PAC-hog Bill Paxon, obtained for us. As if living in the shadow of nearby Attica weren't enough, now we can look forward to playing jailer to frightened Mexicans and angry Haitians who will slit our pale throats once the usual overcrowding sets in. In today's Batavia, even the prisoners have to be imported.

Speaking of our quondam county courthouse (now a historic limestone storage facility), one of my fictive models was the title character in Berry Fleming's charming 1943 novel *Colonel Effingham's Raid.* The Colonel, reappearing in his sleepy Georgia hometown after a long absence, is aghast to find its venerable courthouse on the eve of destruction. Swelling with outraged patriotism, he calls all good men and women to the ramparts. But no one listens, save the Daughters of the Confederacy.

Colonel Effingham had his raiders, and Batavia has hers. They are elderly, mostly women, often delightfully (or maddeningly) eccentric. Their companions live on old shady streets and in cemeteries. They are Friends of the Library and members of the Holland Purchase Historical Society. They remember what Batavia used to be;

they are saddened by its decline, which they cannot prevent. Because the city is no longer theirs.

It belongs to Tops and Kmart and Wal-Mart and Genesee Community College (run by credentialed outsiders) and Taco Bell and Time Warner Cable and the Monroe County Water Authority and the Government of New York and Uncle Sam.

We have been crushed, not by the iron hand but by a soft noiseless Foot Locker sole.

◻ ◻ ◻

I do not want to paint too relentlessly depressing a picture of the Batavia to which I returned. Hundreds still gather for Friday night high school football, though nonrelatives grow rarer in the stands. Dozens attend the Batavia Concert Band performances on summer Wednesdays in the Blind School Park. A hardy band of volunteers mows the grass in our pioneer cemetery. Yet so many more Batavians are huddled around the living room TV, watching *Friends* instead of earning friends, as localism withers on its ancient vine.

All over Batavia, as well as Upstate, people have pledged allegiance to a specious national culture. They are Americans, not Upstaters, and if you believe, as I do, that homogeneity is death, then this loss of particularistic, parochial patriotism is a horrible thing. The provinces ape the capital, which in turn despises them—and do we really need the Eddie Vedder of Glens Falls, the Faith Hill of Franklinville, the Julian Schnabel of Syracuse?

Our region's fey but undeniably indigenous rock band, Jamestown's now deformed 10,000 Maniacs, was better known in Los Angeles than in Batavia. This was a pity, as lead Maniac singer Natalie Merchant is a Burned-Over Chautauqua County spiritualist. An oddball, but *our* oddball.

In all my years of pop culture slumming, I found just one example of Upstate rock and roll regionalism: the liltingly beautiful "New York Country Song" by Syracuse's Todd Hobin Band. Todd and the boys failed to dislodge REO Sludgewagon from late '70s playlists, but their anthem spins on my turntable to this day: "They say down in New York City the people are all cold as ice / But way up in New York Country, the folks are so warm and so nice." Okay, it ain't "Tangled Up in Blue," but it ain't Jewel, either.

I could go on; I *do* go on.

The question I faced, and could not answer until I had been home for a decade or so, was this: How does one *begin* to revive a regional culture long dormant? I used to think it was funny when populists rode into town alone and went out the same way, disgusted that the townsfolk hadn't enough gumption to take up arms. Like when The Clash went to Jamaica to stir up Rasta revolution and found that black audiences wanted "Four Tops all night." But The Clash were interlopers, white men in Hammersmith Palais. Jamaica was not their marrow.

There is an earnestness bordering on the pathetic in those writers who have gone home again. Sinclair Lewis learned his counties but just couldn't stay in any one of them for very long. Jack Kerouac held court at his brother-in-law Nicky's bar in Lowell, Massachusetts; a drunken bum, said his neighbors, just another high school jock gone to pot. Helen Hooven Santmyer published two failed novels and returned to Xenia to teach English. She lived the life of a bourgeois spinster and wrote a fat bestseller, . . . *And Ladies of the Club*, and a loving history of her Xenia, *Ohio Town*, yet I wonder: Did Xenia treat her well? Flannery O'Connor had no choice; lupus chased her back to Milledgeville, Georgia. But even the sainted O'Connor gave in to fitful bitterness. She wrote to an admirer, Benjamin Griffith, "Since you show an interest in my book I presume you are a foreigner, as nobody in Georgia shows any interest. Southern people don't know anything about the literature of the South unless they have gone to Northern colleges or to some of the conscious places like Vanderbilt or Sewanee or W&L."

How I wish we had a Vanderbilt, a Sewanee, a W&L. (Yes, we have Cornell University, if you wish to learn about, say, lesbianism among the Iroquois.) Young southern writers, no matter how remote their parish, how indifferent their neighbors, have a thousand pole-stars of every conceivable magnitude and color to guide them. The clear southern sky is full of William Gilmore Simms and James Branch Cabell and Carson McCullers and Eudora Welty and even glittering Truman Capote, and look, there's the Thomas Wolfe nebula, huge and diffuse.

Upstate, the firmament is cloudy. There are footprints in the snow, but they are unillumined, hard to follow, and most just tail off after a while. The territory is uncharted; trailblazers are bound to get lost in the woods, and it takes years to learn that the lost often make the best findings. You can preach and scream all you like, but certain facts are irrefragable: Batavia is now owned and operated by distant corporations. We are governed by Washington and Albany (in practice, New York City). We read magazines written by corporate outsiders, watch television shows produced by people who despise us, hold jobs on the sufferance of business school–trained executives who wouldn't be caught dead in the best of our restaurants. (Our nouvellest dish is spaghetti, and the traveling company of *Miss Saigon— as seen on Broadway!*—ain't ever gonna grace the stage of the Batavia High auditorium.)

◻ ◻ ◻

At the end of our second year back in Batavia, St. Jerome, the Catholic hospital in which I was born, sought to purchase one of the last mansions on Main Street: the Fisher-McCool home, built in 1811 and used most recently as a Christian Science church. The plan was to knock it down. In its stead would stand a bulky residence for affluent elderly people. An architect from St. Louis with the irritating name of Tyson Trueblood was hired to supervise the razing and subsequent rising.

The preservationists, centered in the Landmark Society of Genesee County, of which my wife would soon thereafter be president, took their case to the zoning board, and lost. Two votes were cast to save the Fisher-McCool home. One was by Catherine Roth—a woman of aristocratic demeanor who is stern to strangers but really a softie underneath. She is honest, indefatigable, and faithful to the old Batavia, despite her origins in pre-malled Long Island. The other loyalist was Hollis Upson, rooted son and heir to a manufactory. The three votes for demolition were cast by Italian-surnamed commissioners. Is that ethnic division significant? Am I bigoted to notice? (A self-hater, as I am an Italian quadroon? Before I am banished to a reeducation camp, allow me to plead for immunity. I am a church-going Catholic—St. Joseph's parish, since birth—blessed with my beautiful and proudly Italian—Northern Italian—grandmother. I assume this pedigree shields me from the dread brand "nativist." No scarlet letters for me, thank you.)

The matter then went to the city council, the court of last resort. Preservationists packed the City Hall chambers, which are located in the 1853 red-brick home of George Brisbane, son of our first merchant and ancestor of the gassy Hearst columnist Arthur Brisbane. City Hall, too, may one day be reduced to rubble, but that fight is for another day.

The *Daily News* set the tone in its pre-meeting editorial: the "Fisher home must go," it lectured, because the hospital is "leading the rush into the future." Hospital officials derided opponents as "history buffs": a devastating put-down in modern America! With dreary predictability, the council enthusiastically approved destruction; we rushed into the future, unimpeded by the past. The Fisher-McCool home came down, and in its place rose the quaintly named "Victorian Manor," with its restaurant "Chardonnay's." Oooh: classy.

The hospital, St. Jerome, later would be submerged within Genesee Memorial after a rancorous merger fight marked by the rawest expressions of anti-Catholic bigotry I had ever heard. Old St. Jerome was stripped of crosses, of statuary, of holy images. Some preservationists took a certain perverse pleasure in the demise of St. Jerome;

I did not. For the sinners were sinned against in turn, and like Jesus, I wept.

But I was in Batavia to stay.

You see, in my irresponsible youth I had cashed a government paycheck as a legislative assistant to Senator Daniel Patrick Moynihan. After almost three years I fled Washington aboard a Greyhound bus for Salt Lake City, where I took a room in a flophouse and wrote derivative Beat poetry and played at stumblebum bohemianism until the daily sight of my neighbor in the adjacent fleabag room, a Manson lookalike who subscribed to *Boy's Life* for the pictures, convinced me to move on. From Mormon HQ I embarked on a circumnavigatory tour of America, to graduate school, to Southern California, to Washington again (for I learn slowly those lessons I do not particularly wish to learn), and then finally to Batavia.

Toiling for a maverick liberal drove me not to drink but to libertarianism, the ideology of legalized dope and criminalized taxation. I still vote Libertarian when I'm not voting Green, but my real party is Batavia First. I would rather edit a booklet on Batavia's greatest architect and excavate the life of a lady painter, my great-grandmother Jenny Garraghan's good friend Ethel Harding Kingdon, or just drive around picking up donated ratty furniture for the historical society's yard sale than rail against the state. I would rather practice an anarchy based on love than preach a sterile liberty.

As a boy I attended John Kennedy Elementary school in Batavia. Its eponym, strange to say, was not the thirty-fifth president and Angie Dickinson floorboard but rather the turn-of-the-century superintendent of Batavia schools, a self-consciously important man who wrote books on orthography and popularized the "Batavia System" of instruction, which he called "a royal road to learning."

Our John Kennedy did not need any reminding that he was a substantial citizen; pomposity bound his books. Yet John Kennedy loved Batavia, and he celebrated its history. On October 13, 1894, in a driving rainstorm, six members of President Cleveland's cabinet dedicated the Holland Land Office museum to the memory of Robert

Morris, patriot and financier of the Revolution. Superintendent Kennedy was lord of the dais, frock coat stretched to bursting, sententious pearls falling from his mouth as the raindrops pelted the puddles. Everyone in Batavia was there, and none more so than Kennedy.

But if our John Kennedy merited every "Kick Me" sticker that irreverent wits pinned to his back, he was *ours*, and the symbol of an age in which Batavians might still organize their own schools and draw up their own curriculum. He was a fanatic on the matter of teaching local history, for as he wrote in his history of the Holland Land Office: "Grandfather's chair may be a very humble piece of furniture, but it is prized beyond all price because it is grandfather's chair."

If Batavia and Upstate New York—and western Kansas and the upper peninsula of Michigan and the Florida panhandle and your home, wherever it is—are to remain distinct entities and not mere wattles on a homogeneous continental blob, then we must remember this.

I will go John Kennedy one further and say that Grandpa's venereal warts should be prized beyond all price because they are Grandpa's venereal warts. Which is to say that even our sins and the pustulant evidence thereof must be preserved in all their local color.

In Batavia, we once had our very own legendary madam, Edna Gruber, who for decades kept a famous brothel, called at various times the Central Hotel and the Palace Hotel, at 101 Jackson Street. (My dad and his pals made Edna the target of many a prank in those blessed days before caller ID ruined juvenile fun. "Edna, this is Ebling Electric. Just calling to see if your blowers are working . . .")

Edna was a foul-mouthed alcoholic old slattern who beat her grandchildren with a baseball bat; she was also the city's most generous philanthropist. Her first husband wound up in Joliet Prison. Hubbie Number Two (Edna slyly listed her occupation as "housewife" on the marriage license) wound up in jail for beating the hell out of his better half and was ordered to "get out of town" by City Judge James A. LeSeur.

Not until her sixth arrest, in 1941, did Edna spend a moment in jail, and the leniency accorded her was due less to the basic laxity of small-town justice than to her benefactions. She endowed the orphanage that occupied the former home of railroad baron Dean Richmond; she paid the medical bills and bought shoes for discalced children; she anonymously donated milk and graham crackers for the students at the largely Italian St. Anthony's School; she paid a priest to buy First Communion dresses and suits for the children of her neighborhood; she quietly distributed dolls and baseball gloves and toys to the boys and girls of indigent parents every Christmas; she bought radios and lightbulbs for the infirm.

Prodded by bluenoses—probably transient Protestant ministers— the cops had to raid her once or twice a year, but she was usually forewarned by her friends in the police department, who included my grandfather, Ed Kauffman. (Believe you me, though: no Kauffman ever paid for it.)

The Methodists and Baptists sneered with all the piety they could muster when in 1953 St. Joseph's gave the old whore a Catholic interment, but a popish wag put an effective end to the controversy when he remarked what a shame it was that so many of her best Protestant customers missed the funeral.

Edna's is long gone; lechery, too, has been abstracted, made unreal. Next door to Edna's old place arrived Batavia's first X-rated video store and vendor of what used to be so charmingly known as "marital aids." So rather than disport with the local doxies, the boys can stop by and pick up a video by which they can jerk off to Los Angeles crack whores and make like Graham Parker: "I pretend to touch and you pretend to feel."

Yes, I know. I am condemning globalized culture by quoting an Englishman whose snarl I heard on a disc of vinyl that was produced by a multinational corporation. I do not claim virginity in these matters, knowing, as I do, the words to the theme songs from both *The Brady Bunch* and *The Partridge Family*. And if I rely overmuch on foreign rock and rollers, well, I understand the attractions of imported culture. After all, my friend Chuck Ruffino and I were Batavia's only punks, circa 1978, affecting Jam-like British accents, wearing our dads' skinny ties, grinning like Nick Lowe and sneering like Elvis Costello, snorting derisorily at our coevals' promotion of Styx, Supertramp, Kansas, and other dreadnoughts of corporate schlock-rock. I was not raised on hearty indigenous fare alone.

But like my heroes—old men who refuse to learn the metric system, wizened spinsters who instead of whining about their goddam osteoporosis write and self-publish books about the grain merchants and farmwives and country doctors who built their towns—we have it within our power to nurture 1,001 little regional revivals. Like the old paper-rock-scissors game, one handful of dirt trumps an entire globe. Or so I tell myself.

Every Main Street and Oak Street and Elm Street deserves its own record, its own poem, and the lack thereof is not the fault of David Geffen or Rupert Murdoch, however loathsome these men and their playthings may be. Kansas realist Ed Howe understood that "in every town there is material for the great American novel so long expected, but no one appears to write it."

The tools of our regeneration are at our feet, if we'd just take a minute to look down. "Art, although potentially universal in significance, is always more or less local in inception," as Grant Wood wrote. Wood painted *American Gothic* for his muse and murals for the amusement of Cedar Rapids businessmen: the perfect synthesis of art and life on Main Street. He did so at the same time Henry Luce and the American Centurions wanted their uppercase *Life* to replace our lowercase lives, and yet we endure. Batavia's Holland Purchase Historical Society recently put together a wonderful exhibit of the work of Batavia's own Grant Wood, the naturalist Roy Mason, kind of a Winslow Homer without the PR agent. Mason, a legendary horn-dog and jokester among the solid men of the Sinclair Lewisian Batavia Club (now on its last trouser legs), supported himself by painting calendar art for Family Liquor Center and the Baker Gun Company, among others. In today's Batavia, Vincenzo Del Plato, our shaggy muralist, our southside Diego Rivera . . . but I am getting ahead of myself. That's in chapter 7.

The great Ed Abbey called his classic *Desert Solitaire* "a tombstone . . . a bloody rock," and he advised readers in those pre-September 11, 2001, days to "throw it at something big and glassy." Some may "love the sound of breaking glass," as a reprobate Englishman (whose wife, Carlene Carter Cash, even more memorably vowed to put the "cunt back in country") once confessed, but rocks are no match for tanks and bombs and organized hatreds.

The colossi of globalism—Disney, the U.N., Time Warner—are impregnable against conventional weapons anyway, so we must preserve our homes, our streets, our Batavias, with acts of recovery, restoration, and resurrection. The seed, the prayer—our only prayer—is love. Which brings us back to John Gardner's Taggert Hodge.

American regionalists face a daunting task. But one thing we must believe. Taggert Hodge was right. Love is the answer. Scrawl it across a highway near you.

CHAPTER TWO

Return to the Natives

Why hasten on;—hast thou a fairer home?
Has God more richly blest the world than here,
That thou in haste would'st from thy country roam . . .

—JONES VERY

Yes, I know that Very was mad, very mad, a Salem quietist given to trances, so strange that he even gave Thoreau the creeps, but there is no more richly blest place than one's own. Be it ever so humble. Batavia may be unlovable, but it is mine. It was mine before I was born, city of my stirps, and when we came home (or I came home, Lucine's childhood having been a blur of California addresses and interchangeable palm-lined avenues), I was determined to fit. Mis-fit, perhaps, but fit somehow.

Coming home. Such a felicitous phrase. But how does one do it? And once the homecoming is achieved, how does the returnee stick it out? After you've alighted from the plane and sauntered down the red carpet—or, more likely, been vomited from the Greyhound in mizzly middlenight—what then?

Why, just fall headfirst into Batavia, my boy.

No less an authority than the Episcopalian Church (a virtually extinct sect that once claimed the allegiance of D.A.R. ladies and parvenus who had changed their names) officially declared Batavia an intellectual backwater in the Algernon Crapsey heresy trial of

1906. Crapsey, a Rochester minister and father of the American poet Adelaide Crapsey, had denied the Virgin Birth, the Trinity, and the Resurrection. This is not far from where Episcopalian orthodoxy stands today, but it was a big deal back then.

A change of venue shifted this ecclesiastical trial of the century to our St. James Church. As historian Karen Alkalay-Gut writes, "It was removed to a sleepy town, where the members of the court were country clergymen, far removed from the influences that were disturbing the intellectual life of the church in great centers. A place more sophisticated than Batavia would have been inappropriate."

The doubting Algernon was found guilty and left the church. Adelaide accompanied her father to Batavia, and left me a poem, "To Man Who Goes Seeking Immortality Bidding Him Look Nearer Home":

Too far afield thy search. Nay, turn. Nay, turn.
  At thine own elbow potent Memory stand,
Thy double, and eternity is cupped
  In the pale hollow of those ghostly hands.

The Crapseys bring us to Henry W. Clune, my Nestor, whom the old infidel Algernon catechized, and who became a model for me as a Repatriated Man of (if you will indulge me) Letters.

I met Henry in the fall of 1990, when he was one hundred years old. I was writing a profile of him for the *Los Angeles Times Book Review*. He had just published his thirteenth book, a collection of short stories, and was grousing that his editor "could better use her ability to edit a seed catalogue." Henry had scotched plans by admirers for a fete on the occasion of his centenary because "they want you on display like the bearded woman in the Ringling Show or the two-headed calf on the carnival lot." (Anachronistic diction is the badge of the longevous. In *Retreat*, Henry's only unpublished novel, a sympathetic depiction of a homosexual Vietnam-era draft dodger and his befuddled middle-class family, an antiwar protester yells to his comrades, "Cheese it, the cops!")

Born in 1890, on the cusp of the Lost Generation, Henry W. Clune was older than Fitzgerald by six years and Hemingway by nine. For the better part of a century—from 1913 to 1969, with sabbaticals for Mr. Wilson's War and one or two other detours—he wrote "Seen and Heard," the most popular column in Frank Gannett's flagship, the Rochester *Democrat & Chronicle*.

In his spare and slack time he wrote six novels and seven books on regional subjects, including *The Genesee* in the Rivers of America series. "I am a provincial by instinct, by design, and by practice," Henry boasted. He stood *on* what he stood *for*: Clune lived in Rochester and the neighboring village of Scottsville, twenty-five miles to Batavia's east, for all but his few wanderlust years. For most of those decades Henry also resided in that most interesting of precincts, the outskirts of fame. In 1921, after a whirlwind courtship, he married Olympic swimmer Charlotte Boyle, daughter of rakish adventurer Joe "King of the Klondike" Boyle, who was the inamorato of Marie, Queen of Romania. The New York *World* immortalized the obscure swain Henry in "The Wooing of Charlotte Boyle" and then anathematized him in "The Shower that Shattered a Mermaid Friendship." (Just a couple of years earlier, Henry had ripped a photograph of Miss Boyle—whom he had never met—from a magazine and pasted it in his scrapbook. He conspired with a friend to bring her to Rochester for a swimming exhibition; they married barely a month after their first meeting.)

Clune's early novels grazed the bottom of the bestseller lists, but luck deserted him at a couple of critical junctures. "I had a lot of near-misses," he sighed. "I'd be wearing diamonds if I had all the stuff they told me I'd have."

Henry's first novel, *The Good Die Poor* (1937), a picaresque tale of a scheming newspaperman, was purchased by Warner Brothers as a vehicle for Bette Davis and Edward G. Robinson—the thought of those two in a clinch defines detumescence—and never made.

His next novel, the prescient political satire *Monkey on a Stick* (1940), in which a platitudinous salesman with a flair for radio runs for president, was praised by Dawn Powell and the Communist *Daily Worker* but otherwise forgotten. When Frank Capra stole the plot for *Meet John Doe*, the resulting legal settlement was a windfall for the Clunes.

Henry's magnum opus was *By His Own Hand* (1952), in which Rochester's George Eastman is transmuted into Alan Wesley, a steel-willed industrialist who enriches a city and smashes its fusty social hierarchy. *By His Own Hand*—Henry had preferred the less ponderous *The Stars Have Monstrous Eyes* as a title—is one of the best American novels of the titanic businessman. (Wesley bears comparison to Dreiser's Frank Cowperwood.) It also inspired Clune to dreams of a fame that never came.

"When I signed the contract at the Grosvenor Hotel," he recalled, "George Brett, the president of Macmillan, said, 'Mr. Clune, if you'll sign this contract we believe we've got the most popular success since *Gone With the Wind*.' "

It didn't happen: Orville Prescott of the *New York Times* dismissed the book as "vulgar petty gossip," and though it was praised elsewhere and sold 55,000 copies, it fell far short of Brett's promise.

In best auctorial fashion, Henry bore Prescott a grudge unto the grave. "It was a hatchet job," he said, and he knew the reason why: "One minor character says she was bored with boys telling her about a Psi U house party at Williams. Mr. Prescott was a Psi U at Williams." On throwaway lines is our history written.

Fortune also frowned upon Clune's fourth novel, *The Big Fella* (1956)—his own favorite—which charted the rise and fall of a rapscallion political boss modeled after Rochester's George W. Aldridge. When Clune's editor Cecil Scott was pushed to the margins with an eye infection, the book's publication was delayed three months. In the interim, Edwin O'Connor's *The Last Hurrah* appeared, and *The Big Fella* would disappear in the shadow of O'Connor's roistering hero Frank Skeffington.

After our first meeting, I returned almost weekly to Henry's home in Scottsville, where we sat in the fire-warmed den under signed photos of such forgotten novae as Gilda Gray (mentioned in *The Great Gatsby!*) and drank martinis mixed by his son Peter. In the early stages of our friendship I had assumed that each visit would be my last, but after a while, six months or so, I gave it no more thought, concluding, on the basis of all available evidence, that Henry would live forever.

No American writer has ever belonged to a place as Henry W. Clune (he was persnickety if one left out the "W") belonged to gray Rochester. His father once lived in the same boardinghouse as did Susan B. Anthony (who was no barrel of laughs, Pa reported). His mother was one of twelve employees on George Eastman's first payroll. Henry's sense of rootedness was as profound as is humanly possible.

"I liked London . . . but it wasn't Rochester," Henry once wrote, seriously. He loved his city, wryly, and with a capaciousness that could take in dowager and racetrack tout. He also possessed the sort of reactionary streak I love: he lamented the loss of "provincial ambiance" that Rochester's corporatization entailed, and in *The Genesee*, he cursed the "motorboats" that had "disturbed the placid waters of our river [and] befouled the air above it with their oily stench."

Carl Carmer, who edited the Rivers of America series, threw a publication party for *The Genesee* at the Batavia Club, Batavia's landmark of prandial Babbittry. Litterateurs clinking glasses in my fair city! But all Henry remembered of the occasion was that the club, housed in the sturdy brick bank at the corner of Bank and Main, was "dull." (In recent years prosperous Italians have made the social catapult from the St. Nick's Club to the Batavia Club. I have thought that it might be fun to take a membership in the club, once I grow fat and placid enough, but I will insist on sitting in the Booth Tarkington.)

Henry lived almost all his life under the charm of the Genesee, which never passes through Genesee County, and along its meta-phorical banks. A verse by the early-nineteenth-century poet William Hosmer, the bard of Avon, New York, seems apt:

> *Ambition from the scenes of youth*
>   *May others lure away*
> *To chase the phantom of renown*
>   *Throughout their little day;*
> *I would not, for a palace proud*
>   *And slave of pliant knee,*
> *Forsake a cabin in thy vale,*
>   *My own dark Genesee.*

Henry cheerfully conceded his parochialism. He loved quoting Bernard de Voto: "Why see Paris, France, if you haven't seen Paris, Illinois?" And he had before him the cautionary examples of his Paris, France–seeing Rochester friends Philip Barry and Louise Brooks.

Philip Barry grew up several blocks from Henry's native Linden Street. An Irish-Catholic boy of considerable charm, Phil left the Flower City for Yale and later George Pierce Baker's drama workshop at Harvard (where Thomas Wolfe was a classmate). He never looked back.

"Phil was a dandy," Henry recalled. *Was he ever.* He married a rich girl, lived in Cannes and East Hampton, and wrote a series of clever drawing-room comedies that made him "a tidy sum of money," as Wolfe noted, not without envy.

Two of Barry's plays—*Holiday* and *The Philadelphia Story*—were delightfully filmed, but except for an anthology edited by Brendan Gill, the playwright rests in obscurity. "Phil is even forgotten in Rochester," Henry used to fret. Barry's sophisticated epigrams and horsey-set badinage are alien to his native soil and simply cannot survive without continuous sunlight from stars afar. Phil Barry didn't need a hometown, and in death, I'm afraid, his hometown doesn't need him.

Louise Brooks staggered into Rochester because she had nowhere else to go. She was a Kansas chorine who made a slew of silent movies, most famously the German G. W. Pabst's *Pandora's Box*, in which she played Lulu, the guileless hedonist, irresistible to men (among others), until, lucklessly, she picks up Jack the Ripper. (Talk about Mr. Goodbar.)

Louise was an erratic, arrogant, dissipated beauty. She slept with everyone except the moguls, and she reviled Hollywood while taking its money. The industry was run, she later wrote, by "coarse exploiter[s] who propositioned every actress and policed every set. To love books was a big laugh. There was no theatre, no opera, no concerts—just those god-damned movies." A has-been at thirty-three, Louise fled the glitz.

She ended up back in Wichita, teaching dance, until a scandal involving the better part of a high school football team made it best for her to move on. She drifted downward until 1956, when she settled in Rochester at the invitation of the curator of the Eastman Museum of Photography, whose archives she mined to write the razor-sharp essays later compiled in *Lulu in Hollywood*.

Louise Brooks and Henry W. Clune began a fitful, exasperating friendship. She swam in gin on dinner dates, Henry remembered, but her bile was . . . bewitching. She lived in a dingy apartment on Goodman Street, paid for by William Paley, an old flame. Henry hated to stop by her tenement because "she'd never stop talking. You could never get out."

(I repeated this to our Washington friend Jay Pascucci, a Brooks fancier. He was aghast. "She was casting pearls before swine!" he exclaimed. I relayed this to Henry. "Swine," he grinned, "oh, that's great. I've been called worse"—not least by Louise, who frequently vilipended him as a "goddamn bourgeois." Henry asked me to extend to Jay an open invitation to "stop by and hear all about Louise. I'll tell him she wasn't any great beauty. She reminded me of general housework." General housework? Cheese it: the cops!)

Louise reentered the Celebrity Nation in 1979, thanks to Kenneth

Tynan's lengthy paean in *The New Yorker*. European cineastes had long insisted, "There is no Garbo! There is no Dietrich! There is only Louise Brooks!" Finally, cisatlantic adulation was hers. She died in 1985; four years later, Knopf published Barry Paris's 609-page biography. "Mose," Henry growled, his saltiest epithet. "Six hundred pages for an actress? That movie *Pandora's Box* bored me to tears."

Henry showed us some poison-pen billets-doux he'd received from Louise in her last crippled years. Brooks soaked even her Christmas cards in vitriol: under the stenciled "Season's Greetings" her chicken scratch lacerated Humphrey Bogart ("a gentleman and a bore") and Will Rogers (a stone drunk whose companionship all avoided: "No wonder he never met a man he didn't like"). She even slagged the man who had resurrected her reputation. ("Tynan was no fag—just your usual upper-class English pervert.")

Louise refused to indulge Henry's provincialism. "I hated you," she reminisced fondly in one Christmas letter, typically devoid of Christian charity. Henry was too . . . "Rochester." She airily dismissed Clune's claim that his friend Phil Barry was the equal of O'Neill and Coward. She reviled Rochester as her Coventry. "To be a rebel is to court extinction," Louise once murmured in a self-dramatizing fog. For all her tartness and capricious debauchery and undeniable pulchritude, I wonder if she ever realized that Henry, doggedly and faithfully creating a Rochester literature of place, was more of a rebel than she ever dreamed of being.

The elderly dine on tales told twice times twenty, and Henry was no exception. But I did enjoy hearing about his rescuing Babe Ruth from a Geneva whorehouse, or about the herpetophiliac saloonkeep "Rattlesnake" Pete Gruber and the elegant stripper Hinda Wassau. Not to mention his days running around with a young stagestruck George Cukor. (Henry had a certain willful imperceptibleness. After reading Patrick McGilligan's *George Cukor: A Double Life*, for which Henry had been a source, he remarked to me, "I never knew George was a pansy.")

Every few months Henry and his bon vivant son Peter threw a

party. Lucine and I dressed as though we were about to step into a Marquand novel—she a knockout, me slightly askew, tie loosely knotted. The room filled with ghosts, octo- and nonagenarian wraiths of the old Rochester, men whose names were on venerable commercial enterprises, women born to industrialist fathers, tennis-playing gamines turned white and wrinkled, if often charming. George the barman poured, as he had since before the Flood. The gin in those martinis could pixilate a linebacker. One December evening, as the snow covered the cars in the drive, I had three too many. I staggered to our maroon Chevy Celebrity and fell asleep in the passenger seat. Lucine eased it onto the North Road, its farmhouses like lighthouses every mile, and as the snow whitened the unplowed lane she heard a rude hiss from the left front tire. Gamely, without help from the snoring drunk next to her, she guided the lolloping Celebrity ten miles into the parking lot of the McDonald's in Le Roy. Whereupon I opened my door and vomited, much to the amusement of the loitering Le Roy youth.

Lucine called Dad from the McDonald's phone, accepting the commiserating grimaces of those cashiers whose off-hours are spent enabling their spouse's alcoholism. Mom and Dad drove the fifteen miles through the snowstorm; Dad changed the tire as the ejecta froze to my chin. They drove us home, and helped me up the stairs and to bed. I awoke the next morn, remembering little. Lucine, still mortified, provided the grim details. Mom, over the phone, said only, "We were not proud to be your parents."

O, for the anonymity of the manswarmed city!

Not every young man in the prime of his hardihood can be drunk under the table by a 103-year-old, yet on my every crepuscular visit Peter mixed the gin and vermouth, and I struggled to keep pace with my seniors. Peter was an interesting case. He was (and is) natty, a red hanky always blooming from his jacket at table. This dapper dan was also a dinnertime diseur, a charmer with a prodigious thirst for gin. Peter had studied at the American Academy of Dramatic Arts, as he was not loath to mention. His tuition had been paid by the

Woodwards, the Le Roy family that bought the patent for Jell-O for $450 from a penniless tinkerer named Pearl Wait. The Woodwards amassed a fortune, and Pearl Wait entered the pearly gates penniless.

Peter Clune had something of an erratic career, playing character parts on the stage, lending his roundly handsome face to numerous print ads, and acting in a cluster of B—no, C—movies that he has done his best to conceal from me. He owns up to the minor, often nonspeaking roles: one of the guys at the subway command post in *The Taking of Pelham One, Two, Three*; an Irish something or other in John Huston's virtually unseen *Sinful Davey*. But for me, Peter is best loved as the Max von Sydow to director-writer David Durston's Bergman. The best-known film in Durston's exceedingly odd oeuvre is *I Drink Your Blood*, in which a band of homicidal hippies eat rabies-tainted meat pies and, well, turn rabid. This was too infra dig for Peter, but he did appear in such Durston productions as *Blue Sextet*, one of the first films to earn an X rating. According to *Variety*, *Blue Sextet* features LSD, suicide, and "a ghoul defil[ing] a naked woman's body." Video distributors, get cracking! Peter also made a mark in Durston's immortal *Stigma*, the flick that launched the soon-to-crash career of Philip Michael "Miami Vice" Thomas. In this oddity, which the *New York Times* unaccountably called "a crackling good suspense melodrama," Peter played a bigoted New England sheriff who gives an entire island the clap. The movie, available on video, is atrocious, not even fun as camp, and when finally we persuaded Peter to watch it—alone—he emerged from the experience dazed by its ineptitude.

However, our Peter Clune film festival does contain one jewel—Allen Baron's *Blast of Silence*, the early '60s neo-noir cult favorite in which Peter is a mob boss targeted for a hit. Reputations have been made on less. (We are introduced to Peter in *Blast of Silence* when the hitman studies his snapshot and the hardboiled narrator growls, "You know the type . . . a mustache to hide the fact that he has lips like a woman. The kind of face you hate.")

Henry also reveled in the low end of showbiz: burlesque palaces were a favorite beat, and he would compose comically purple odes to their voluptuous denizens. Yet he never really acknowledged Peter's career. I don't think he even believed that Peter was *in* movies and theater. These suspicions would have been confirmed had he lived to see one of Peter's most recent modeling jobs in the Rochester tentacle of the Gannett Octopus. The ad read, "I Lost 26 Lbs! It took less than 4 months—my doctor was delighted and amazed . . . Peter Klune [*sic*], Actor, Pittsford [*sic*: Pittsford is a tony suburb, evidently classier in the adman's mind than quiet Scottsville], Results Atypical." As well as indiscernible, for I had seen Peter the previous month and not noticed a significant subtraction from his modest avoirdupois.

Yes, Willie Mays ended his career misjudging fly balls for the Mets. I popped in our bootleg video of *Blast of Silence*, among the grimmest of noirs: that really is Peter, Henry. He really was an actor. And he was *good*.

"I've had a wonderful life," Henry often said, as he sat in his den, fire crackling, drinks poured, lights on high, urging me to read Marquand, read Macaulay, read Hemingway (the short stories). He was lucid till the end; a few days before his death he called to urge me to "read Zola." A Francophobe, I still have not; sorry, Henry.

Three weeks before his death, I gave a talk at the Richmond Library on "The Life and Work of Henry W. Clune." Peter drove Henry to Batavia; Henry shuffled in, crouched over his cane, and sat in the front, probably hearing about half of what I said. He had often asked me to give the eulogy at his funeral. I thought of this as a dress rehearsal, with the guest of honor open-eyed. I was admiring, and sincerely so, in my talk. He was pleased.

Within a month I reworked the tenses and gave much the same talk at Christ Church Episcopal on Rochester's East Avenue. Standing in the same pulpit from which the bishop had once denounced the heretic Crapsey, I offered Carl Carmer's poem about an old farm couple:

Late June he died
"Don't mourn," said she,
"Things keep on
That folks don't see."

But Henry was something of an egotist, and I knew that he'd be peeved if I didn't quote from his own work. So I concluded my remarks with Henry's valediction from his penultimate book, a memoir:

> I have known no great triumphs. Flowers have not been flung in my path; I have heard no cries of "Viva!" But I have done almost everything I wanted to do. In the vespterine quiet of a warm summer evening, on the terrace in front of our house, I have occasionally heard a whispered query: Where would you rather be than here? The answer is prompt and inevitable. Nowhere else in the world. Except for a couple of departures in early manhood in futile quest of greener pastures, I have lived all my long life no more than fifteen miles from the place of my birth; thirty-seven years in the city of Rochester, fifty-five years in the same house with the same wife in the village of Scottsville. I always had a lurking wish to appear considerable in my native place, and in a career of nearly three-score years in the newspaper business in Rochester I achieved status and a desirable prestige. I always liked it here.

And "here" always liked Henry.

❐ ❐ ❐

Unlike most writers, Henry W. Clune was not the perpetual outsider looking in, the stranger even at home. I envy his absolute sense of belonging. Lord knows I'm not there yet. For every time I settle too complacently into my role as Batavian, I get jolted as rudely as a David Durston hero confronting rabid meat pies and the clap.

False Memory Syndrome is endemic to the memoirist. Recollec-
tions of four-touchdown games and passionate couplings with cheerleaders flood my unreliable memory. But whene'er I am tempted to
bathe in the warm misremembered glow of a Batavia adolescence—
what's too painful to re-me-eh-ember, we simply choose to forget—
I call to mind the twentieth reunion of the Batavia High School Class
of '77.

A Saturday night at the Batavia Holiday Inn. I wear a tie, Lucine
is pretty in blue. I am nervous. Debbie Heath, the organizer, was one
of only six black girls in our class of 250+. The daughter of Reverend
Heath, she is currently studying for her Ph.D. in Rochester, which
will make her the only member of the Class of '77 to have the hon-
orific "Doctor" before her name (other than a chiropractor who lost
his license for sticking his finger up a teenage girl's ass while bab-
bling about "past life experiences"). Debbie greets me warmly, even
though I don't think I had a class with her since first grade. This is
reassuring. Still, I need a drink. Janet K., always two seats behind
me in the *K* row of homeroom, approaches. Her dad had been a
muckamuck at the Eaton factory that employed my dad before the
goddam Nazis ran it into the ground.

"If it isn't Bill Kauffman."

"Hi, Janet. Great to see you."

"Oh yeah, you too."

"Janet, this is my wife, Lucine."

"Hi, Lucine"—I like to tell people that Lucine is Armenian for
Darlene, but the joke always falls flat—"nice to meet you. Bill, this
is my partner . . . Susan."

I am flabbergasted. It truly never occurred to me that an actual
lesbyterian might have attended BHS. We chat for several minutes.
They live in Seattle. Janet is now Janet K.-A., she talks about "married" life. I congratulate myself on my suavity, and how liberal I am
for a reactionary. I had quite forgotten Janet K. but I find myself
liking her very much, admiring her guts. (They are, needless to say,
the only such couple present.) Afterward I regret not talking to her

and the missus at greater length, but this is not possible at reunions, as I discover.

Things go downhill rapidly. Hey Bill. Hey Tim. How ya doin? Not bad. You? Pretty good. Twenty years, huh? Yeah, man, twenty years. Hoo. Again. And again. Or worse, simple nods of semi-recognition. Sometimes not even that. Here and there more than five words are spoken: to the formerly obese Roger, who has slimmed down and has a girlfriend and a motorcycle. I want to hug him and tell him I've thought about him, as I have thought about so many of these strangers, and tell him how happy I am for him, but instead I pump his hand, as the primeval high school fear of acting "weird" reasserts itself. I have a pleasant chat with Mitch, the only Jewish boy in our class—now the richest, it seems.

At the sit-down dinner, I whisper to Lucine, "Let's get a drink." The plan is to grab my thirty-second beer and park ourselves near the bar, so my classmates can pay homage. We get the beers. And stand. Alone. Lucine snickers, then breaks into a laughing jag. Several minutes go by. Unvisited, I slink back to the table, a prophet without honor.

All night long I wanted someone to be honest, to realize that We May Never Pass This Way Again, as the '70s prom warhorse went, and to share the lessons of two decades in a spirit of boozy fraternity. This is what I have done; this is what I have learned; may I see your road map?

But a reunion demands that you pick up where you left off at seventeen, which is why when the dinnerbell rang the Class of '77 split into what bitter girls used to call "cliques." Tables formed around jocks, the pretty Italian girls, the vivacious girls, the guys who had pubic hair at twelve and went on dates when they were fourteen, etc., leaving the rest of us, the great unaffiliated, to scramble for the odd vacant chair.

For a moment the clouds break. I hail Jean, one of the cutest girls in my class. Hers is a farm family rooted in the black soil called muck—yeah, yeah, mothermuckers, all the little muckers, etc.—but she lives in Seattle. (Was it the Perry Como song that lured these Batavia lasses to the city of corporate-marketed grunge?) "Hi, Bill." She remembers me. Despite my intoxication I summon a few drops of wit from the reservoir. Then a wave of sentiment engulfs me.

"Y'know, Jean, in third grade you performed some act of kindness toward me, I forget what, and so I have always been fond of you."

She giggles. "Oh, I can't tell you my memory of you. It's so embarrassing." I assume that it involves something clumsy or mortifying on my part, like the recent day I spent interviewing and tailing Mayor Giuliani only to find, at day's end, that a piece of toilet paper had been sticking from my rear pant-waist since early morning.

"I was so naive about things," she begins. "I didn't know where babies came from or anything, and in fifth grade all I wanted to do was sit behind Bill Kauffman because I thought that's how I could have your baby."

This, I must tell you, I will remember. Yes, it came twenty-five years too late, but still. I tell her that when we were in third grade, I had a bit of a crush on her, and there was this song by Rod McKuen (for purposes of memoir, I should change this to the Velvet Underground and "Venus in Furs")—Jean, Jean, you're young and alive . . . Bonny, bonny Jean.

"To this day I think of you when I hear that song."

We chat for a few minutes more. She tells me that she "builds power plants" or somesuch, and I keep my anti-nuke mouth shut. This is what I wanted from the reunion.

Lucine and I drift out of the Holiday Inn. Roses are not strewn in my path. The totality of my eclipse sinks in, depresses me. Fifth grade is gone. All is decay and loss and finally death. Memory is cruel. It promises things that never were delivered.

"My people." Yes, I know all about the unspoken things, the language of the inarticulate, but what if the silence signifies . . . nothing? Janet K. is now the un-Batavian, I am the Ur-Batavian, yet why do I feel more comradely toward her than toward the volk? I realize, at this and other odd moments of a lifetime, that my love for Batavia will ever be unrequited. Cherish is the word I use to describe . . .

We do not attend the next morning's breakfast at the Holiday Inn. The blue and white balloons have been popped, the message board no longer welcomes the BHS Class of '77. The people who live away will drive to the airport today. The bluest skies you've ever seen are in Seattle . . . Twenty years is a very long time. Jean, Jean, you're young and alive . . .

All this I perpend.

Oh cheer up, you goddam sadsack. You may have moved back home but that doesn't mean that the old hometown has to assume the smooth factitiousness, the bland inauthenticity of a TV movie, just for your sake.

For what is more nauseating than the fulsome home-ism of a song like Bing Crosby's "Dear Hearts and Gentle People," in which Der Bingle, between cuffing some sense into his son Gary, croons about a hometown filled with dear hearts and gentle people who never, and I mean never, let you down.

What horseshit. Sung by a true faithless ex-son of Spokane. Batavia will *always* let you down, you can never depend on it, but it's home, and that has to be enough.

◻ ◻ ◻

Ideally, in the Batavia of my dreams, the high school would bring us together.

Yet the utter spiritlessness of BHS never fails to amaze. Not to sound like some glee club wuss, but not once in my high school years did we sing "Ever Batavia," our mordant alma mater. ("Ever Batavia thy spirit shall stand"—if not thy buildings.) Even the jockocracy was unhonored. Don Bosseler was the only NFL player Batavia ever produced. An all-American at the University of Miami, he was a running back for the Washington Redskins for eight years in the late '50s and early '60s (before white running backs became as scarce as black lepidopterists). Bosseler graduated from Batavia High in 1953, but I'd never have known if Dad hadn't told me Paul Bunyanesque tales of Dashing Don: why wasn't his number 31 on display in the underfilled trophy case?

Given all this and so much more, it came as a befuddling surprise when the *Daily News* reported in early 2001 that "a leading provider of information about places in the United States has completed a ranking which reveals Batavia is one of the best hometowns in New York State—a leader in hometown spirit." The source of this startling news was ePodunk, an Ithaca-based company. Batavia earned its merit badge by virtue of the stability of its population: its blessed immobility. It seems that we move around less than the people of any other small city in the state. Batavians stay Batavians. And yet these tenacious roots seldom reveal themselves in public debate.

Even as ePodunk's computers spat out our glory, the school board was voting, with but one objection, to color our new outdoor track red instead of the cyanic hues of the Blue Devils, the gormless nickname adopted by clueless schools across the land in the midcentury ultimo. To add insult to injury, the high school graduation was transplanted from its traditional site, under the weeping willow in front of the high school, to the auditorium of Genesee Community College. The sole dissenter on these matters, the jots and tittles that give our lives a theme, was Alice Ann Benedict, older sister of my chum Tom Holvey. Alice Ann is a former BHS cheerleader, Class of '72, who married the quarterback, Wayne Benedict. She laughs that she has been "teased mercilessly" for caring about the color of the high school track, but sometimes surface appearances reveal a good deal about what's underneath.

As we sever every tie to our past, as the last of the old stores close, as the grand old homes are razed or vinyl-sided, as the landmarks that are vested with memory-made myth disappear under the junk heap, how much longer can we stay atop the ePodunk honor roll? When everything you knew is gone, why stay?

My pal Mike Sheehan is thinking about getting out. Mike's mom, Rosalyn, or "Mammo," hailed from deepest darkest Blackshear, Georgia; Mammo's mother had the inimitably perfect name of Fleader Mobley McBee. The beloved Mammo supervised our underage drinking, limiting us in her husky cigarette-cured voice to no more than two or three Gennys and a swig or two of malt duck as we played blackjack into the night, Sheehan and Chuck Bobo and I, dateless, eating the pizza made by Nancy Arena's brother Jerry. Ah, those were the days.

(Mike is responsible for one of the great moments in Batavia youth baseball. His team of nine- and ten-year-olds was whipping its foe, 17–3, when Mike called for his pitcher to issue an intentional walk to the other team's best hitter. The rival coach called time out. "I don't believe it," the coach yelled at Mike. "I've never seen an intentional walk in this league. And you're ahead 17–3!" True enough, Mike conceded. But a home run would make it 17–4, and who knows what might happen after that?)

Mike tends bar at the Elks Club: the Benevolent and Protective Order of Elks (B.P.O.E.), or as my dad and his pals used to roar half a century ago, Biggest Pigs on Earth. If Rotary is about networking, and Kiwanis and Lions are about service, the Elks have a narrower purpose: getting drunk. Mike was recently made a Lecturing Knight, which means, as he explained to me, he gets "lectured to at night."

Frank Homelius, the junior partner in the father-son architectural dynasty that designed so many of Batavia's finest buildings, was an active Elk, and the run-down headquarters on Main Street retains a shabby dignity. Mike and I clutch our Gennys and we josh each other in the obscure language of old friendship.

Mike talks about moving to Florida with his girlfriend once his youngest boy graduates from BHS. Nothing for him here, he says: he works at Chapin's, last of the nineteenth-century family-run manufactories, which is in the same shape as most northeastern manufacturers in the age of NAFTA and GATT. His folks are dead, a sister and brother are already basking in the Sunshine State: Why stay?

"I'd miss you," I mumble, and the truth is I would. For what is Batavia without its Sheehans? Porch-sitting (under the black POW/ MIA flag, for the oldest boy was in Vietnam), beer-drinking, Van Halen–cranked-up-listening Sheehans: my Batavia, scattered to the continental winds. Don't go, Mike.

He hasn't yet, but that's because he has a sentimental streak.

◻ ◻ ◻

Like some vanishing North Dakota hamlet deciding not to be, Batavia is losing people. From a peak of 18,210 in 1960, bolstered by a newborn Bill Kauffman, we have shrunk to 16,236. If the hospital closes, as rumor and fate suggest, several hundred of its almost 1,000 employees will leave, including the foreign doctors who play no part in civic life (but whose progeny keep Batavia High stocked with valedictorians). While Genesee County's population hovers around 60,000, the number of 25- to 34-year-olds plummeted by 31.5 percent between 1990 and 2000.

Upstate New York was among the biggest population losers in the 2000 census: we rivaled western Pennsylvania, eastern Ohio, and hardy perennial West Virginia in lost people. Given that we are a virtual colony—King Numbers dictates that statewide politicians are all downstaters—we lack the right to self-determination. Politics offers not even a pull-away hand to grasp at from the quicksand.

As Norman Mailer said in his 1969 candidacy for mayor of New York City (he proposed to cut loose city from state, bless him) in what may be the greatest American political speech since William Jennings Bryan's 1896 "Cross of Gold" oration:

> Our authority has been handed over to the federal power. We
> expect our economic solutions, our habitats, yes, even our enter-
> tainments, to derive from that remote abstract power, remote as

the other end of a television tube. We are like wards in an orphan asylum. The shaping of the style of our lives is removed from us—we pay for huge military adventures and social experiments so separated from our direct control that we do not even know where to begin to criticize. . . . So our condition is spiritless. We wait for abstract impersonal powers to save us, we despise the abstractness of those powers, we loathe ourselves for our own apathy.

Or is apathy just another word for being wise enough not to waste effort? In the spring of 2001, red splotches appeared overnight on most of the street-side maples in Elba, my Batavia-bordering exile. Our friend Marty Stucko, the only Elban with a "Nader for President" sign in his front yard the previous autumn, advised that these towering old trees were targets not for pruning but razing by Niagara Mohawk, the western New York utility monopoly. I called Elba's mayor, who confirmed Marty's suspicion. The trees were goners. The mayor ended our conversation with a plaintive, "You can't fight City Hall," meaning Niagara Mohawk, an interesting comment on the relative might of local governments and corporations.

"Oh yes you can," I replied, mustering all my blowhard vainglory, and after a day of furious EarthFirst! reveries about spiking trees (which I wouldn't know how to do anyway) I drew up a plan. Not a good plan, in fact a bootless plan, but a plan.

The first step: the posting of a poem! After all, the pen is mightier than the sword, and presumably the chainsaw, too. So I copied George P. Morris's nineteenth-century classic "Woodman, Spare that Tree" and stuck it on the Elba Post Office bulletin board, the corky village green.

Woodman, spare that tree!
Touch not a single bough!
In youth it sheltered me,
And I'll protect it now.

The power monopolists stood firm. A call to the Cooperative Extension Service put me in touch with a "certified arborist," who hazily agreed to come out in "a coupla days" (but never did) to assay the health of the threatened trees. They looked hale enough to me; in fall, they made an orange-yellow-red canopy at our end of Chapel Street. But these brazen maples had the effrontery to predate the utility poles and the taut black lines whose juice makes possible such marvels of the modern age as VH-1, the automatic dishwasher, and the star-erasing night light. (These poles are cruciate in form, you will notice: the cross of the Religion of Techno-Business.)

My calls to the state's Public Service Commission inevitably produced the pulsing busy signal; in frustration I sat down and wrote an angry but reasoned letter to the CEO of Niagara Mohawk, forgetting everything I had learned twenty years ago about the futility of "writing your congressman." *They do not care!* I never sent it, opting instead for the personal touch: first a visit from a smiling Niagara Mohawk tree man, who commiserated with me on what a damn shame it was, and then spray-painted one more tree just to teach me what happens to those who fuck with NiMo. Pathetically, under cover of night I went out and spray-painted the red blotches gray. Yes, the Resistance was in high gear!

I needn't bore you with the details of my futility. Down they came, seven of the eight street-side maples within a 50-yard stretch. If only 'twere pulp fiction.

But you see, the mayor had a point: you can't fight the boardroom. Oh, you can beg for mercy, or call in nonexistent chits, or fall to your knees in Lewinskyish supplication, but if you fight you will lose. The town of Elba was at the same time being sued by a cell-phone company. It had refused the invaders permission to erect a 200-foot tower at Elba's entrance: our very own barbican. Members of the board discovered, to their surprise, that it is actually illegal for localities to spurn the Cell-Phone God. And like Mailer, we loathe ourselves for our own fugging apathy.

Not that local politics can't be amusing or eventful.

"Every vote counts." The sanctimony with which the networks' unsinkable anchors intoned this numbing platitude in the wake of the Gush-Bore tussle of 2000 had to chaff even the most naive civics teacher's ass—no statewide election in U.S. history has ever been decided by a single vote. But locally, the canard metamorphoses into a truism. In the mid-'90s, Cindy, a friendly congregant of Lucine's Presbyterian church, ran for the Elba School Board. She was one of five candidates running for two available seats. Usually I bullet-vote—that is, vote for a single candidate rather than the two I am allowed in such races. I pulled the lever for Cindy (no chads hereabouts) and was about to draw back the curtain when I decided aw, what the hell, I'd vote for the guy I reckoned on coming in last. I have a soft spot for losers, for the rejected, for the man who dresses up in a chicken suit all day promoting a new fast-food joint and then has to come home after a long minimum wage workday and face his adoring daughter, lint from the chicken head curled round his collar.

Well, it turned out that Cindy won 104 votes, which tied her for the second and last seat . . . with the very popular guy for whom I had cast a last-minute pity vote. Oh my. A runoff was held, and this time Cindy lost outright. I never told her that my impetuous act had cost her the race—how could I?—though I do comfort myself by thinking that if I hadn't done my capricious bit she'd have been injured in a car accident whilst driving to or from a Board of Education meeting.

So at the most local level—swallow the bromide.

Lucine and I have run for no offices, but we are on boards; oh are we ever on boards. Lucine, or "Lupine," as spell-check (evil invention) insists on correcting her name, is the off-and-on president of the Landmark Society of Genesee County, and though I am a director I am more the Denis Thatcher than Hillary Clinton consort type. The Landmark Society was the nobly powerless organizational critic of urban renewal thirty-five years ago, and in the years since it has done the Lord's work in recognizing restorationists and providing a means by which like-minded folk can talk cornices and entablatures. It is politically impotent, of course: "Remove not the ancient landmark which your fathers have set," says Psalm 22, but that was expunged from Batavia psalters by an impish Rotarian.

I am also on the board of directors of the Holland Purchase Historical Society, the Batavia Muckdogs, the Friends of the Richmond Memorial Library, and I suppose the John Gardner Society, although in a spirit of Gardnerian anarchy, we've never gotten around to doling out titles, offices, or personal parking spaces.

A single minute spent hearing the minutes of a last meeting or a treasurer's report uplifts me; this is democracy and civic-mindedness on the human scale, without glamour or power plays (well, for the most part). Unlike vicarious charity (write a check, receive a computerized thank you, deduct it from your 1040, and pretend it matters), volunteer labors at the grassroots really do bring forth tangible, audible results. The exhibit of paintings by the Mason family; the preservation of the St. James Episcopalian church rectory, which would otherwise have been demolished; the John Gardner readings every October; the return of minor league baseball every June: these are the doings of the men and women on these and fifty other boards, the corncob nobility that keeps Batavia Batavian. Just as valuable are those who act their parts with utter un-self-consciousness: the arthritic jock, cowled in windbreaker, watching from on high in the Woodward grandstand as BHS tackles and stumbles through another fall; the prematurely gray sot sucking Gennys at noontime behind the shades in Kelly's Holland Inn; the crabby old crone with a "No Peddlers or Solicitors" sign in her front-door window, despite the fact that no Fuller Brush Man or footsore encyclopedia salesman has disturbed her avenue since LBJ was president. They, too, sing Batavia, if not in dulcet tones.

Ideologies wither and die in the climate of the civic association. I learned this when I was asked several years ago to serve on a grant-making panel of Go-Art, or the Genesee-Orleans Regional Arts

Council, which disburses perhaps $50,000 annually in public monies to artists and organizations in our two counties.

"Uh, okay," I replied, forgetting that several years earlier, I had written for the *Wall Street Journal* and the libertarian Cato Institute in opposition to public funding of arts and artists. My objection was not based in Helmsian prudery (though I am as one with the most pervervid defenders of the faith when subsidized bohemians and trust-fund trash immerse crucifixes in their syphilitic urine or cover the Virgin in cowshit) but rather in the belief that bureaucracy stultifies. As John Sloan said in 1944, "Sure, it would be fine to have a Ministry of the Fine Arts in this country. Then we'd know where the enemy is."

I had published a single novel and was thus a Novelist—The Novelist Bill Kauffman, speaking with the same ex cathedra authority as The Novelist Ivana Trump or The Novelist Ethan Hawke. Under the Cato Institute's auspices, I appeared on fifty-plus radio shows and spoke at fora from Chicago to Chattanooga, having a grand old time turning the tables on the pious PBS-watchers who were my debating foils. Joseph Epstein once called me "quotatious," and I suppose I am: I read off the roll call of American critics of government-funded art—Faulkner, Emerson, Vidal, Updike. Standing on my side were Paul Goodman and Lawrence Ferlinghetti and Larry Rivers; your side had Lyndon B. Johnson and Archibald MacLeish. Let's rumble.

But I was not about to explain to the bright and hardworking Kelly Kiebala of Go-Art that my Thoreauvian anarchist principles forbade me from sitting on her panel. I justified myself to myself with the usual sophistry: Go-Art is financed by the state and county and does not receive loot from the real enemy, the National Endowment for the Arts, which supports (1) urban museums and symphonies whose patrons have average incomes far higher than those of the average taxpayer; and (2) the sandbox tantrums of rectum-obsessed performance artists who mock rural and working-class people (and who exhibit less diversity of opinion than the congregation of a 1950s Kansas Methodist church).

So I went. And I was so impressed by the artists and schoolteachers and housewives who took very seriously the job of doling out a thousand or so dollars—the staff of life—to the Genesee Symphony Orchestra (GSO), the Genesee Chorale, photographers along the Erie Canal, and muralists in brick village downtowns that I have agreed to serve every year since. No, I have not taken any public money, not even for my bicentennial play: I do have my principles. But if they flex now and then, I chalk it up to the exigencies of small-town life.

We're awful proud of our symphony, as Wilder's Stage Manager would say. Founded in 1946, it's the oldest community orchestra in the whole United States. (A kid named John Gardner, a French horn player from the Putnam Settlement Road, was a charter member.) The GSO plays four concerts a year; past conductors, like the present one, the ebullient Raffaele Livio Ponti, have usually been Rochester or Buffalo based.

Midsized cities like to boast of their symphony orchestras when recruiting midlevel managers (when the managers would really rather hear whether or not county laws require the placement of G-strings at local strip joints). But the GSO draws respectable crowds of several hundred at a time when orchestras in far larger cities of putatively greater sophistication have long since closed shop. I don't know why, except that Batavia schools have fine music programs. Men who wouldn't cross the living room to insert Mozart in the CD player will go to the symphony of a Saturday evening. For two hours once every season Batavia assumes the rhythms of a middle-class city out of Henry Clune: I can't shake the feeling of displacement, as though I've stepped into the wrong time and place, but it's a pleasant sensation nonetheless.

The GSO does not play native compositions: unlike the summertime Batavia Concert Band, the orchestra has never played "The

Batavia March," composed by the great Roxy Caccamise, evangelist of the accordion and the John Philip Sousa of Genesee County. But then neither are the Muckdogs locals, and in their three-score years they, like the GSO, have developed a distinctly Batavian crust.

◻ ◻ ◻

The country lawyer turned Upstate memoirist Bellamy Partridge, a Hobart man, wrote that by the first years of the twentieth century "the American country town began to lose its flavor, its individuality, its peculiarities of local custom and local idiom. It was no longer the product of its own environment. Outside influences were now directing its growth and development. The great god Regimentation was in the saddle and ready to go."

My God, Partridge, that was a century past. Are we to just give up the ghost, buy Nikes and Britney Spears albums at Wal-Mart, and join the Army or Microsoft, as though there were a real difference?

The mobiles have won. They dominate every potent institution in America. The stay-at-homes, the sluggards, the boys and girls who "ain't goin' nowhere," have lost. Or have we? In *The Portrait of a Lady*, Henry James had Henrietta Stackpole define a "cosmopolite": "That means he's a little of everything and not much of any. I must say I think patriotism is like charity—it begins at home."

Just so; which is why we placeists cannot but loathe the blinding stars in our political firmament, those placeless beings whose password was spoken by Newt Gingrich, who once replied, when asked his provenance by a fellow grad student, "I'm from nowhere." As is New York's junior senator, former First Lady Hillary Clinton, who is so anchorless that she ran for office in a state in which she had never lived. But, the cosmopolite will gleefully interject, she won! Yes she did: she won handily the ultramobile precincts of the cities, and lost badly in Genesee County, trounced by her callow foe Rick Lazio, baby-faced focus-group creation on the GOP line.

The Newts and Hillarys, the Bushes and Gores, have won, at least by their generally accepted accounting practices. But they have no homes, no place that has to take them, in Robert Frost's phrase, and we do. That counts for something; in my book, it counts for everything.

When I was a boy, our next-door neighbors were Joe and Eleanor Dougherty. He was an amiable toothless drunk, a rum-dum, as my grandmother would say, who told us he had once played for the Rochester Red Wings. She was Irish and Catholic and friendly and long-suffering. One day the Doughertys were sitting in our living room; Joe was gurgling down Gennys, the mild intoxication deepening his usual deafness. He smacked his lips after a particularly satisfying slurp. Eleanor said to us, with a love-worn fondness: "Look at him over there. He's not much, but he's better than nothing."

In a world of widows, bereft and adrift, Batavia is my Joe Dougherty. This is such an unlovely place yet I love it with all my heart. To visitors, it is a charmless Thruway stop on the Rust Belt's fringe; to me, it is the stuff of myth and poetry, and of life weighed on the human scale—the only measurement that counts.

CHAPTER THREE

We Want a Hit!

I grew up one block from Dwyer Stadium. The park was known as MacArthur Stadium until wiser heads renamed it for the shoe store owner who kept baseball in Batavia rather than the West Point left fielder turned general who may have returned to the Philippines but never set foot in our town. The stadium name will not change again—at least not as long as those who remember Mr. Dwyer, a white-thatched old gent with no kind words for umpires, are alive.

Batavia is an anachronism in the suddenly chic world of minor league baseball, wherein teams are bought and sold as briskly and thoughtlessly as one plunks down a red hotel on Baltic Avenue. We shamble on, safe from plucking by thirtyish bond traders trying to impress their girlfriends or *Saturday Night Live* has-beens eager to purchase regular-guy cachet. Batavia remains a community-owned franchise in the gold rush that has become the New York–Pennsylvania League, colloquially known as the NYP.

What was once a compact league based in the small cities of western New York, northwestern Pennsylvania, and southern Ontario—Olean, Wellsville, Lockport, Welland, Bradford, Little Falls—now sprawls into such godforsaken reaches as Vermont, New Jersey (New Jersey?), and Ohio. Imagine our dismay as the NYP has been invaded by Ben & Jerry's–slurping Lands' End–cowled e-trading Burlingtonians, Youngstown mafioso, and the people who gave us Jon Bon Jovi.

Ours used to be a league of virtuous little towns right out of *It's a Wonderful Life*, which was set in west-central New York. The NYP's recent helter-skelter expansion has been enough to drive Jimmy Stewart over that bridge, Clarence the Angel be damned. As generations of young Batavians have said in that Italianism that no one has yet bothered to translate, *"meenga fotch."*

The New York-Penn, né PONY (Pennsylvania-Ontario-New York) League, is the nation's oldest continuously operating Class A league, yet its very name is now obsolete. There are more teams in Massachusetts than in Pennsylvania, and new clubs have been placed in Brooklyn and Staten Island, of all places. But Batavia hangs on, rich in lore if not purse.

We were one of six original teams in the PONY League, whose organizational meeting was held at the Batavia Elks Club. Dan Winegar, the late *Daily News* columnist, loved to tell of the inaugural game on May 10, 1939, when 3,000 fans rimmed the field, many sitting on folding chairs supplied by Batavia's funeral homes, as the home club was buried by the visiting Jamestown Ponies.

The team was christened the "Clippers" in that inaugural year. In a midlife crisis it adopted the name "Trojans," reclaimed the "Clippers" in the 1980s, and then became the "Muckdogs" in the factious fall of 1997. I still slip and refer to our team as the Trojans, a name derived from Trojan Industries, maker of bright yellow tractors and quondam employer of my father and hundreds of other Batavians. At least until Trojan was purchased by a German concern in the early '80s. Upon taking possession, the new German owners, displaying the puckish humor and gentle mercy for which their people are so widely loved, fired all salaried employees who were within a few years of a full pension.

They did so without repercussion, for unlike the Batavians who had once owned Trojan, our Teutonic overlords were tied to Batavia only by the flimsy cord of the almighty dollar. The executioners did not have to look into the faces of fifty-year-old men, good and loyal workers, solid fathers and citizens, who were handed their walking papers one week before Christmas. A couple of years later, the Germans goose-stepped out of town, leaving an empty factory and devastated lives in their wake. We had lost our Trojan war.

Dad may have worked for Trojan, but his heart had always belonged to the Clippers. He sold Cracker Jack, shagged foul balls, and served as batboy in the 1940s. I filled Dad's cleats on a fistful of occasions, my service as batboy regent arranged by a gangly pitcher with black horned-rim glasses named Joe McIlvaine, who at a precociously young age became general manager of the New York Mets. Both Dad and I are now benched, but I never tire of hearing of his boyhood heroes, especially Moose Kromko. (Among my favorite curios is a scored program from the 1945 championship game against Lockport in which Moose Kromko homered.) This pillar of the sporting life was a barrel-chested second baseman who spat contemptuously at batters reluctant to swing, "Whaddaya want, egg in yer beer?"

When my father tried that line on my grandmother, a proper Irish-Catholic, he learned the wisdom of Charles Barkley's contention that professional athletes ought not to be role models.

My dad was an industrial engineer, but he began his working life as a railroad man, a surveyor for the New York Central, the once-mighty line that the Vanderbilts stole from Batavia's sole titan of industry, Dean Richmond. I shudder to think that the capricious hand of fate (and the conniving cupidity of Commodore Cornelius Vanderbilt) deprived Batavia of its own Gloria Vanderbilt, but then Richmond had a knack for betting on the wrong horses. As Democratic chairman of New York State, he orchestrated the 1864 nomination of General George McClellan to oppose Abe Lincoln, which is why his name was tarnished (and his mansion demolished) in our fervently Unionist county.

All of which is to say that my dad is no misty memoirist or

baseball-moistened intellectual, à la George Will, whose boyhood probably was spent in right field praying to the Virgin Mother to ward off pop flies.

Dad has never eulogized the *timelessness* of the game, or composed georgic odes to the way it embodies the agrarian rhythms of nineteenth-century life. Yet Dad, who once boasted (falsely) to me that he had never read a book in his life, recently drew up a four-page reminiscence that he titled "MacArthur Stadium, Batavia, NY: My Playground From 1944 Through 1956." Without an adjective in sight, he lists his jobs—selling peanuts, popcorn, and Cracker Jacks; shagging fouls; groundskeeper; batboy—and calls out the roll of summer names (Batavians, mostly, fans rather than players). Now and then he pauses for a recollection.

"We had a lot of fights while shagging balls," he writes. "The game would start with about a dozen baseballs, and if it got down to eight Don LaBrussa would come out and yell at us." Or "If it rained before the game, the low spots on the infield would fill with water. One man would drive to Herb Acheson's gas station on Bank Street for two five-gallon pails of gasoline. We would pour gasoline in the water holes, light a match, and burn the water off." He mentions briefly that his Notre Dame High School team also used the field, though characteristically he does not note that he was the first Notre Damer ever cited for the Western New York All-Catholic Baseball team. He concludes, "In the winter we would jump off the grandstand roof into the snowdrifts in front of the grandstand." These are real memories, not purchasable by Mastercard.

My favorite story of Dad's, the kind to be filed under "Lore," I suppose, comes from a game played in dense fog in the late '40s. The Clippers had a wily right fielder. His name is lost to time; let's call him RF. On air-thick nights our hero was wont to sneak a game ball out to his station in the late innings. Be prepared, as the Boy Scouts say, and on this evening RF was. As the night wore on, the murk became almost impenetrable. "Can't see a thing out there," muttered fans and players. In the top of the ninth, a slugger for the opposing team drilled a rising liner to right. The ball was lost the moment it left the infield. All eyes shifted to RF as he drifted back to the fence and leaped, glove over the Iroquois Beer sign. How deft his theft! His athletic leap was followed by a graceful two-feet landing, then the jubilant waving of his gloved hand above his head as he sprinted to the infield. The ump signaled out. The crowd was incredulous: this was the catch of the century! That ball was arcing four hundred feet on the fly! "Goddam fog musta kept it in," was the favored explanation. The next morning my dad walked on the hillock behind the right-field wall, and in the glistening dew he found a brand-new PONY League baseball.

Time does not befog baseball memories. I have spent so many hundreds of hazy summer nights in the bleachers, watching Batavia play through a series of affiliations (Pirates, Tigers, Indians, Mets, Phillies) while compiling one of the worst cumulative records in the history of the minors. We have won but three championships—in 1945, 1946, and 1963—no easy task in a league that has had as few as six teams.

All minor leagues, including the NYP, take great pride in the players they've fed to the big leagues. Pete Rose first bowled over catchers in Geneva. In 1973, Robin Yount was a seventeen-year-old shortstop for the Newark Co-Pilots (that's Newark, *New York*, apple orchard country). NYP grads served up 22 of Mark McGwire's 70 steroid-fed home runs in 1998.

And on it goes, round and round the diamond. I've fond memories of seeing a handful of journeymen you've never heard of (John Knox, Jerry Dybzinski, Bernardo Brito) begin careers that ended somewhere between their first major league at-bat and Cooperstown. Don Zimmer, the coach memorably dubbed "the Gerbil" by his Red Sox pitcher Bill "Spaceman" Lee, helped the Hornell Dodgers to the 1950 PONY League title. ("That little railroad town was a hell of a baseball town," the Gerbil cheeped to a Rochester sportswriter in 1999.)

Our boys have even tackled the National Football League. In

1982, a Stanford quarterback named John Elway, with rodentine if not gerbil-like dentation, hit .318 over one autograph-filled half-summer with the Oneonta Yankees, and in 1998 the Muckdogs had a dreadlocked left fielder named Ricky Williams, who left town after a month to return to the University of Texas and a Heisman Trophy–winning season. Williams couldn't judge a fly ball to save his life, but he was, as they say, quick down to first.

Before my time in the bleachers, future Pirates Steve Blass, Manny Sanguillen, and Dock Ellis filed through Batavia. So did expansion-team fillers Cito Gaston and Woody Fryman. I dimly recall, at the dawn of my own historical memory, complaints about "too many blacks" on the team, which must date to the mid-'60s affiliation with the famously polychromatic Pittsburgh Pirates. Gene Baker, manager of Batavia in 1961, lived down Bank Street; he was the first black manager in the history of (non-Negro League) professional baseball. An ex–major leaguer, Baker was treated as a celebrity, or at least as much of one as a person who lives in a tumbledown walkup on rundown lower Bank can be treated. We are, you will recall, descendants of the rural abolitionists of New York's Burned-Over District, and our Presbyterians and Methodists and Episcopalians have long been afire for equality of the races, at least so long as the races stay out of Genesee County.

A later black manager, the onetime Pirates second baseman Dave Cash, met an ignominious end. He and his wife came to town in the summer of 1990, and Mrs. Cash made an immediate impression. She was *not* pleased to be exiled to the bushes. (Once you've tasted Pittsburgh, I gather, all else is gruel.) At any event, early in July 1990 manager Dave Cash was reassigned to the uncoveted position of "roving infield instructor" after what the Batavia *Daily News* primly referred to as "recent incidents involving his wife, Pamela."

The incident that cashiered Pamela's husband—and sent the glorious name of Batavia through the wires to every *Post* and *Gazette* across the land—came in the early innings of a Monday night game against the despised Oneonta Yankees, perennial NYP champs.

On that *USA Today*–making day in July, Chipper the Clipper, the Batavia mascot, a sort of home-sewn San Diego Chicken—I shan't torture you with fowl puns—was flapping through the grandstand, shaking if not baking, when he committed the lèse-majesté act of wiggling his chickenish backside in Mrs. Cash's face. Feathers promptly flew. Mrs. Cash launched a profanity-laced tirade that set a still-unsurpassed standard of ballpark billingsgate. A day later, Dave and Pamela bid farewell to our town. "He shook his butt in my face," said an unrepentant Pamela Cash, "and it wasn't the first time."

Players come and players go, usually with less fanfare than the Cashes, but it is the fans, passing lifetimes in the bleachers, who give minor league baseball its sense of permanence. I have seen the same faces since my childhood: the longtime club president was Dr. Laurence Roth, Catherine's husband, retired ob/gyn and violinist-trombonist in the Genesee Symphony Orchestra and the Sousa-philiac Batavia Concert Band. The vice president is Jerry Maley, a second baseman for the Batavia team in 1948–1949 and my Babe Ruth League coach. (If only he'd been a more astute judge of talent and installed me at my natural shortstop position instead of the Siberia of left field.) Mr. Maley was also the first high-schooler ever to hit one out of MacArthur.

The club's directors tend to be shopkeepers, doctors drawn from the dwindling pool of American-born M.D.s, and independent craftsmen ranging from barbers to contractors. The game-night program used to include brief bios of the Batavia Board of Directors. For instance, the 1973 general manager was limned, "Sports is his diversion—Insurance his bread and butter." Our favorite began, "A clothier by trade . . ." and we snickered at the starchy prose. The clothier is retired but still in the stands each night; his family haberdashery is closed, as are all the men's wear shops but one. Pushed by The Gap into the abyss.

I look around the third-base bleachers, my home away from home. There's John Hodgins, county legislator and landscape artist. Mr.

Hodgins paints the ads on the outfield walls. Dennis Bowler drives a tractor across his family's small farm before motoring down from Niagara County to watch a farm team of a different sort. Sardonic old Merle wears a hat that says "Mr. Grumpy" and greets slumping bonus babies with a cheerful cry of "You're due, hot dog!"

Merle's fellow hecklers have largely died off; I miss the sour old man who yelled, "Why doncha change your name to E6?" after the shortstop—our shortstop—had bobbled yet another grounder. When the kid flashed him a glare, the gruff geezer hooted, "Pay attention to the game, rabbit ears!" His successor is another older man in a blue windbreaker who abhors taken pitches and erupts, with enviable satisfaction, "*That*'s what happens when you swing the bat!" whenever a Muckdog hits a home run.

This is the cast that has enriched the summers of my life. The ensemble is not changeless. At each season's end I know that come next June, another face or two will be missing from the bleacher tableau. This past year the absence was Harold Alwardt, retired custodian and longtime scoutmaster, who yelled "Hey rothead" at any umpire who dared call a close one in favor of the visiting team.

A demotic ethic is at work in the bleachers, where a cop and a tree surgeon, a mini-mart cashier and a chiropractor, groan at bum relievers and homesick .177-hitting Dominican shortstops. The box seats that line the field cost just a dollar more per game than the bleachers, so the boxes are no gated community, though they are the seats of choice for the doctors and lawyers: the graduates of Cornell, the Oxbridge of the Upstate cowtown aristocracy. The doctors and lawyers smile benignly upon one and all, but I have never heard one of them yell at an umpire. Such vociferating is left to the working class.

The umpires in the NYP league are barely older than the players. The median age is perhaps twenty-four; they work and travel as duos in lonely vagabondage. I remember in 1994 when a brush-cutted ephebe of an ump threw out Mike O., a hotheaded Clipper with the sullen good looks of the petty larcenist next door. Mike performed his tired bat-throwing "Fuck!" routine after a called third strike, and the ump waited until the volcanic whiff artist had returned to the bench to give him the heave-ho.

"What?!" screamed Mike, racing back on the field to protest his ejection. "You don't have the balls to kick me out to my face?" We were then privy to every glower and cower, as the ump's blue-clad authority vanished and he stood there stricken, lost, with the fear-frozen mien of a third-grader who finds himself alone with the class bully within a circle of jeering schoolmates. It was one of those rare moments in professional sport when the crowd is jolted to sense. Even in the lowest minors, the players are a self-aware Elect. Take the most piggishly arrogant cheerleader-mauling jock you knew in high school and multiply him by fifty, and you've got a professional athlete.

Mike revealed himself as a nasty bully—without the Olympian detachment of the more typical jock, who doesn't bother to pick on retarded boys and fat girls but would never dream of defending them. As a result, he lost the crowd, which began to vent tentative boos in his direction. He then flipped us the bird and stormed to the club-house. I imagined the young ump brooding at Dunkin' Donuts into the wee hours of the morning, wondering what perverse ambition led him to be unmanned in front of nine hundred residents of a town so prideless that it tore down its Main Street.

It takes only a verse or a chord for me to revive the dead of Dwyer. Just a snatch of a song that used to chirr over the scratchy PA system while groundskeeper Stevie Roth was dragging the field and Trojans were playing pepper. Maybe it's "Roll out those lazy hazy crazy days of summer." Or Mungo Jerry's "In the Summertime." In morbid reverie I see them once more. There is Cider Barrel bellowing at the umpires; Jim Pangrazio holding his cup of beer in the hand with three missing fingers; Pete Severino, classmate and friend, who tried to retrieve a stranded Frisbee from a tree with a metal pole and was struck dead by the telephone wires.

Dad used to point out the toothless hag who, in more toothsome days, had shared her youthful charms with the players in the '40s and the pleasures of her maturity with the coaches in the '50s. I tried to picture her as a looker but suffered a failure of imagination, and now she is gone to that dimly lit tavern in the sky.

The pop culture nightmares that have filled the place where our memories ought to be are no help in conjuring her. Forget *Bull Durham* (1988), Ron Shelton's much-praised reel of hokum about life in the minors. I know, Shelton was a bush-leaguer himself (a second baseman with the nearby Rochester Red Wings of my youth). But his poetic groupie, played by Susan Sarandon, rang as false as Robert De Niro's rubber-armed catcher in *Bang the Drum Slowly*. In her youth, the raspy-voiced, wizened crone of Dwyer may well have been prettier than Susan Sarandon, but the chance that our Batavia ballgirl ever read Blake between scores is remoter than Pluto. (Still, ballpark venery has never gone out of fashion. Last summer, my dad, walking through the high grass surrounding Dwyer, spelunking for foul balls to give my daughter, found a ball that had obviously come from the bullpen. In relief-pitcher penmanship, it was inscribed to some nameless beauty: "I'm AVAILABLE. Let's meet at Days Inn Lobby 1 hr. after game #? 'Its just for a couple a drinks.' " Whether player and fan met I do not know. The fact that the ball had been discarded in the weeds suggests that our Lothario may have struck out.)

The bullpen pickup artist's grammar was as precise as that of a retired English teacher when compared to the dispatches from the *Muckdog Gazette*, the semi-regular newsletter of the spirited Batavia Muckdogs Booster Club (of which I am a proud member, though not editor). Typically, the newsletter lists "Paided Members," though in defense of such cacography Andy Jackson once said that any man who can spell a word only one way has got to have something wrong with him. Last year's end-of-season number reported, "A lot done this season, Booster Plague Installed on front of Dwyer Stadium as you enter the Park, Ed Dwyer Plague, and Phil Zipkin installed."

The plague was going around last summer, I guess.

And Phil Zipkin was inhumed as well as installed. Phil was the Jewish junkman whose yard was a long foul ball from the playing field, the genial fixture who motored around Dwyer in a wheelchair since "the diabetes" cost him a leg. He was an inverted scalper, which is to say he passed out free tickets just outside the gate to anyone who looked vaguely familiar. Such a nice old man, and I shudder to think that when his unamputated person used to walk past, berobed in a windbreaker reading "Batavia Waste," my wise-ass teenage self used to mutter, "You said it."

Along my third-base bleacher perch sits Albert, the man of lumbering gait whom my dad and his teenage pals used to look out for. Now he is gray and old, even slower of step, but still here, laboriously keeping score in his notebook in a hieroglyphic I never have been able to decipher. He pedals to the game on his three-wheeled bike, which he padlocks to a STOP sign. Almost every September, after the season ends, Albert writes a letter to the editor of the *Daily News* in which he announces that because the management has mistreated the fans in unspecified ways, he will never again attend a Batavia baseball game.

The first time I read Albert's annual abjuration, I was immensely saddened, filled with the usual patronizing solicitude. "The poor old man, that's all he has—what will he do?" And then June came, and Albert was there, scratching his scorebook for another season to be capped by another end-of-the-season renunciation. Albert is just funny that way, I guess.

The slow, the touched, the pixilated, are represented disproportionately among Batavia fans. There is Mark in his bright red Batavia Clippers Booster Club jacket; he speaks so painfully slowly that a sentence stretches into an inning. God bless the Muckdog with enough decency and longanimity to submit to his well-informed conversation. Then there is the fellow with the severely compacted phiz whose name I have never learned but who doggedly delivers advertising flyers to half the doors in Batavia. There is the slovenly and somewhat sinister-looking man I have always, to my discredit, referred to as "Goober." He is tall and unwashed, silent and unshaven, and looks for all the world like a child molester. God forgive me, but he gives me the creeps.

Then there is Ricky. He was always assigned to the slow classes in school, despite his savant's knowledge of baseball and hockey statistics. I have never for a moment believed that his IQ is under 120.

Ricky has been a fixture at Batavia sporting events for all my lifetime. Thirty years ago, he was the ballboy for the high school football team; now he bears the title of "equipment manager," buckling helmets and spitting in his trademark staccato "les go les go les go." In the YMCA basketball league, teenage Ricky used to stand under the opponent's basket while his team was back on defense. A rebounding teammate, if in a generous mood, would hurl the ball court-length and Ricky might pick up a garbage bucket. A stalwart of the Muckdogs Booster Club and member of the board of directors, Ricky sells programs at Dwyer; he looks like a perpetually distracted Fred Flintstone.

"Whaddaya think about the Bills?" Ricky asks along about mid-August.

"They better get rid of [Fill in the name of the Buffalo quarterback of the moment]," I reply with the certitude of the former substitute lineman on a 2–6 Pop Warner team.

Ricky and I nod sagely. Ricky is the luckiest of men: he has a niche, he is an irreplaceable piece of our town. My Batavia without Ricky is unthinkable. Of how many men can that be said?

◻ ◻ ◻

Batavia plays in the McNamara Division, namesake of the late Vincent M. McNamara, the longtime NYP League commissioner. Vince died in June 2000 at the age of ninety-two. He was a hoar-headed old Irishman, and I remember seeing him sitting in Mr. Dwyer's box seat. I heard tales of Vince's swashbuckling from a third white-haired son of Eire, the garrulous Ray Doody. Ray, former vice president of the team in its incarnations as the Clippers and Trojans, ran Doody's Sweet Shoppe on Main Street in Batavia, hiring the pretty high school girls to work the counter. When the malt-shop business curdled, he became a smooth-talking car salesman more oleaginous than a can of Quaker State.

I liked Ray very much. He used to drop into Perkins every Sunday morning to have a cup of coffee with my parents and me after 7 A.M. mass at St. Joe's. "Haya doin' Ray?" my father would ask. In response, Ray would inevitably gust, "It's a war zone out there. It's a war zone." Ray was drinking buddies with Monsignor Schwartz, and was our Cadillac-driving padre's most tenacious defender against criticism that he had reneged on his vow of poverty. (Monsignor Schwartz appears in John Gardner's *The Sunlight Dialogues* as one of the priests at a funeral who "came over from their Cadillac, blessing the crowd." I once asked the Monsignor, after an amiable half-hour inquisition into my lackluster Catholicism, about his cameo in *The Sunlight Dialogues*. He was delighted to be invited, as they say.)

But then the Monsignor dropped dead on an August afternoon. He was a desultory taker of his heart medicine, because, as Ray said, "the bastard thought nothing could kill him." Ray mourned—until the will was read, and Ray made not even a cameo appearance. There were plausible explanations: no doubt the Monsignor assumed that he'd outlive a contemporary who had recently survived a multiple bypass. And Ray was fairly well-off for a mick.

But oh, the fury of a friend unbequeathed. One Sunday morn, fresh from a mass said by Schwartz's successor, the imperious if holy Monsignor McCarthy, Ray slid into our booth at Perkins and observed that it was a war zone out there. Then he shoved a photocopy of the Monsignor's will under my nose. I looked, furtively and shamefully, but I looked. To this day, I regret it. But I looked. Hell, everyone in town looked. I can't tell you what I saw, else Monsignor Schwartz will devise some unusually cruel torments for me when I join him in Purgatory. Suffice to say that he may have shattered a priestly vow. Or two.

Two and a half years later, when Monsignor McCarthy, tenor cracking, said over Ray's body at his St. Joseph's funeral service, "It's a war zone out there, Ray," I could not stanch the tears that wet my cheeks.

Ray gossiped like a fishwife, and his scuttlebutt about Vince McNamara tied the NYP League commissioner to Batavia's cultural arbiter, the ageless Wanda Frank. For decades, Wanda held artistic court with her *Frankly Speaking* morning show on Batavia's sole radio station, WBTA 1490.

With the clear diction of the classic old-school radio elocutionist, Wanda told her listeners of goings-on on Broadway, in Hollywood, in the world of letters. She often directed the Rotary Club's annual musical. She tirelessly promoted local artists and musicians. (Thanks to musical instrument salesman Roxy Caccamise, Batavia was the accordion music capital of New York.) Best of all, she issued ex cathedra pronouncements on matters cultural. *Man of La Mancha*, the latest Tom Tryon novel, *Georgy Girl*—all were grist for Wanda's wonderful mill.

Thirty years ago, when I was home from school with a dubious case of the sniffles, I heard her review of Sondheim's *A Little Night Music*. It was one of her signature moments. Wanda had just returned from her annual trip to Broadway, 400 miles and several light-years distant from Batavia. She played "Send in the Clowns" in its WBTA debut and pronounced it one of the most perfect songs ever written. But she wondered why the new generation of the Great White Way had to spoil shows by using naughty words. This was a Frank bugbear. During taped summer interviews with performers at the suburban Buffalo theater-in-the-round called Melody Fair, she gently chided them—in just-us-show-biz-vets chaffing—for using blue language when so many good clean jokes were available.

In the early '90s, Wanda had asked me to stop by her apartment to sign a copy of a rural New York travel book I had written. How I wish I'd gotten the culture treatment in her heyday! Alas, Wanda had been fired—let go, they call it, like a spaceman from his tether cord—when the station was sold to a cost-cutting Irishman from Hornell. I told her I was sorry she was no longer at WBTA, and that Batavia had been richer for her efforts. "They didn't even give me a 'blanking' gold watch," she said, and in case I hadn't heard right she repeated, "They didn't even give me a 'blanking' gold watch."

I smiled, dumbly. I'd published a novel in which the word "blank" is a virtual article, but I'd never heard it from the lips of a sixty-something lady. After murmured condolences I edged toward the door. Wanda, however, would never be far from the spotlight. After enrolling at Genesee Community College, she resurfaced as director of a student production of *Our Town*. A fine effort, and Lucine and I congratulated her heartily. She graciously accepted our praise and mentioned that she'd previously directed the play for the Rotary Club in the 1960s, and that Thornton Wilder had sent her a telegram of the "break a leg" variety. It was pasted in her scrapbook. I wanted to hug her then and there, but of course I did not. I shook her hand and left her to bask in the approval of the crowded lobby.

Ah, but we have drifted far from Vince McNamara. This is how Batavia is: you can't tell one person's story without bumping into someone else's, and then you introduce the fellow brightening the corner of the second story, whose trail leads across town, down the decades, and back to where we started. One cannot—at least I cannot—tell of Batavia any way but discursively.

So to finish with Vince McNamara. A Buffalo boy by birth, the NYP League's commissioner had been a principal opponent of placing a dome over the stadium Buffalo built for its Triple A franchise in 1979. "Fellas," he told the Citizens Committee of the Erie County Sports Board, "this has to be an open-air stadium with natural grass. That's the way baseball was meant to be played. You don't want to play under a roof and on a pool table." And thus was built one of the finest ballparks in America.

God rest your soul, Vince, and may Batavia ever reside in the McNamara Division.

❏ ❏ ❏

I have shared long wisecracking Dwyer evenings with friends since I was eight years old. Someday we'll all be interred within hailing distance of each other. I like to think that unlike the regret-filled corpses of Wilder's Grovers Corners, we'll reminisce unto eternity about the time Brian Lambe stole home in the bottom of the ninth.

Just as my parents took me and my brother to the games—where we sat behind the Batavia dugout and chanted "We want a hit! We want a hit!"—I take my daughter, Gretel, and we sit with my parents along the third-base line. I am too old and far too self-conscious to chant, or yell anything beyond "Throw him out!" when an opposing manager tiffs with an umpire. But I can fill Gretel's ear with names (where did you go, Dave Bike, Sneaky Grady, Jim Wosman, Dusty Dustal?) and bribe her into baseball with hot dogs and handshakes with Maxwell T. Chomper, the Goofy-knockoff Muckdogs mascot.

Alas, baseball has lost its hold on the younger generation, who are being led into the tedious hell that is soccer. Once the leathery symbol of British imperialism, this damnable sport is now the badge of submission to the Disney state. Nike is spending $50 million on Project 2010, its iniquitous plan to soccerize American youth within the decade. Baseball is fast losing the suburbs. All hope for resistance to a soccer-ball globe lies in the Batavias, in the SUV-less lands where NPR is so much nighttime static.

Any appeal for the preservation of small things, like Batavia baseball, runs into the buzz-saw claim that one's memories are fraudulently idyllic. C'mon, wasn't the GM a chiseler and the slugging first baseman a date-rapist? Wasn't the drunk belching at the ump behind the Batavia dugout a wife-beating lout instead of a lovable Dean Martin sot? Weren't the racist fans harder on black Alex Johnsonish players who dogged it than they were on white laggards? (Maybe yes to the last two.) And—inevitably—that *Leave it to Beaver* world doesn't exist anymore, if it ever did.

These weary and worldly put-downs are made, you will notice, by people whose only knowledge of Middle America comes from the TV screen, which is why they frame their arguments with Hollywood referents. They know nothing of America's Batavias, only the parodies of small-town life that they have watched on the idiot box. To them, our fathers are Robert Youngs and our mothers are Donna Reeds. "Aha!" they shout, in a case-closed voice. "Your idyllic little world is a lie! Robert Young was a suicidal drunk, and Donna Reed's life was the same blur of abortions and divorces and infidelities as that of the next starlet-slut. So cut the pastoral crap!"

Yet the world in which homesick shortstops from Texas gave worshipful kids from Batavia cracked bats and pinches of Red Man in return for dixie cups full of lemonade really did exist. And it still exists, no matter that the image now cries out for a sardonic punch line. It exists because for all of Batavia's failings, baseball is still played and life is still lived here in a personal way.

I do not mean to suggest that Dwyer Stadium is a cloister within whose walls we are safe from the People in Gray and the forces of rampant homogenization. Between every inning, between every batter, between every pitch, it seems, corporate Muzak product erases the silence. The premise behind the ubiquitous pop-rap-rock at ball games is that baseball is so stupefying that only constant aural stimulation can keep the spectator alert. Old men grumble, the middle-aged carp, the young sneer, and the heathen rage, but still the Muzak comes.

The straw that broke my camel's back came in 2001 when manager Frank Klebe bolted from the dugout, charged the ump, and unloaded a Niagara-quality torrent of profanity punctuated by arm-chopping gesticulations. It was a managerial tantrum, one of the most entertaining moments in sports. Alas, it was mere pantomime to those of us in the bleachers: the disc jockey in the press box drowned out the sounds of baseball with "A little bit of Mary . . ." Men who watch MTV should be barred from employment in the minor leagues.

Fans in Batavia, Butte, Grand Rapids, Clearwater—all are assaulted by the same snatches of music, the same petrified gag lines from *Seinfeld* and *Cheers*, the same sounds of flushing toilets and belches that amuse morons from sea to dimming sea. But then baseball, as we are told by unpoetic souls, is Big Business, and what Big Business needs is the standardization of markets.

In fact, we almost lost our team in the early 1990s, when the Professional Baseball Agreement stamped a single cookie-cutter mold over more than 150 American cities and their ball clubs. The PBA covered every last niggling detail of running a team—clubhouse showers, parking lots, lighting, the size of the locker room. Every last idiosyncrasy was smothered.

Purse-poor Batavia did its best to comply. The clubhouse was expanded. The dirt and grass got a manicure. An electronic score-board that malfunctions regularly replaced the old manual score-board to which kids would run between innings to hang the metallic hits, runs, and errors shingles. A boy's life knew no greater thrill. I still hear the bullpen pitchers hooting "Move it Move it Move it" like Gomer Pyle's drill sergeant on those rare occasions when I hung the score.

These changes were not enough. Next, the parent Philadelphia Phillies demanded that Dwyer be reconfigured to more closely resemble Philadelphia's circa 1970 Veterans Stadium, with its boring symmetry. The problem, you see, is that Dwyer's quirky contours made it a hitter's park. The power alley in right-center measured barely 350 feet, and, for half a century, batters delighted to watch long pop flies turn into home runs. Aided by the short fence, Tim Glass, the hulking brush-cutted catcher, hit twenty-one home runs in 1977, a league record that still stands.

The fence, alas, stands no longer. It was pulled and stretched until 1993, by which time it looked like your typical Philadelphia slob, fattened on mounds of inedible cheese-steaks. The Glass record will never be shattered.

Yet even this contortion was not enough. Dwyer Stadium's eldritch, dark green wood grandstand was the product of local workmen, built under the aegis of FDR's Works Progress Administration. It was as sound as most quinquagenarians. But the word came down from Philadelphia: raze the grandstand and the wooden first- and third-base bleachers or lose the team. And so Dwyer Stadium, handicraft of our grandfathers, was demolished, and upon its ruins rose a concrete and plastic edifice called . . . Dwyer Stadium.

To give the devil his due, in 1992 veteran minor league scout Bob Miske critiqued each of the NYP's ballparks. He said of old Dwyer: "The mosquitos will just eat you alive. I mean they're as big as dive bombers. That stadium is falling apart, also. You get a lot of homers in the power alleys because the outfield boundary is kind of square instead of bending out." NYP League president Bob Julian hardly demurred. He remarked, "We have facilities that are either historic or dumps, depending on how you look at it."

I have no doubt how Mr. Julian looked at it.

The other Batavias of the NYP League either dug deep to buy the wrecking ball or lost their teams. Auburn, home of "the worst ballpark in the league," in Miske's estimation, spent $3 million and saved its team. Elmira redid Dunn Field and lost its Pioneers anyway. Geneva, the town in which Pete Rose first bloomed, lost its Cubs several months after its general manager told a reporter, "Basically, we're in pretty good shape." Poor Niagara Falls, erstwhile honeymoon capital of the world, now known as the shabby gateway to the Canadian casinos, decided to pay its firemen rather than rebuild Sal Maglie Stadium, named for the menacing beanball specialist Sal "the Barber" Maglie.

I felt a funny kinship with the Niagara Falls Rapids, né Pirates, all those years. With the clamant obnoxiousness of pubescent punks, my friends and I used to ride a hotshot Niagara Falls pitcher named

Rick Honeycutt. This was so sterling a player that on his days off, he batted in the designated hitter slot, which I have never again seen a pitcher do. Honeycutt's girlfriend—or was it his wife?—sat nearby, her blond prettiness and ridiculously unattainable status no doubt egging us on.

"Honeycutt sucks," I hollered wittily at the close of one game, whereupon Honeycutt's sucker (at least in our lurid imaginations) sized me up and cut me down. I can't even recall her withering remarks, but I was of course rendered quite speechless: no girl this pretty had ever said hi to me, let alone upbraided me. I slunk away, the jeers of my pals echoing all the short way home.

Ever since, Shep and Sheehan and Ruffino and Wolff have ribbed me about Honeycutt's girl, whose boy went on to one of the longest middle-inning relief pitcher careers in major league history (twenty-one years, with a record of 109–143).

But Niagara Falls told the majors to take a hike, and the Rapids swiftly departed, leaving only a rumored cataract to draw in the tourists.

❐ ❐ ❐

Entering the new if hardly mosquito-less Dwyer in June 1996, sitting on its modern plastic seats, I understood for the first time Nathaniel Hawthorne's puzzling declaration, "The hand that renovates is always more sacrilegious than that which destroys."

I detest theological baseball writing as much as the next regular guy, but you don't have to buy *Bull Durham* "church of baseball" humbug to believe that a place at which the generations have gathered in seasonal fellowship is made holy. Or that its defacement can be called an act of desecration.

But I had accepted the post–Vatican II warehouse edition of St. Joseph's after old St. Joe's was burned to holy cinders by certain Italian parishioners who lit the wrong sorts of devotional candles. So I made my peace with the new Dwyer. I came to terms, gradually, with its blue plastic backrests and chain-link fencing and incongruous southwestern brown-brick facade. I had to. The renovation saved our team.

Further salvation came in the form of a Muckdog, a thitherto unknown breed of canine whose litter glitters if not with gold then at least with federal reserve green.

"Clippers," Batavia's nickname on and off since 1939, entangled us in copyright problems with the Triple A Columbus Clippers. (The latter are a George Steinbrenner property, with all the litigious propensities that implies.) Besides, the nickname came not from the nautical daydreams of landlocked Batavians but rather from the harvesting machine, the "Clipper Combine," manufactured by Massey-Harris, Batavia's chief employer in 1939. But Massey-Harris pulled out of town in 1958, leaving vacant an enormous and grimy plant across Harvester Avenue from our pioneer cemetery. From atop his cenotaph, Captain William Morgan glares accusatorially at the empty factory, for the Clipper Combine is deader than Batavia Masonry.

So in 1997, the club sponsored a "Name Your Team" contest. More than 1,400 entries suggested everything from "Bees," the moniker of Batavia's semipro team of the early 1930s, to "Mighty Tonawandas," my own modest attempt to honor the carp and Coke bottle–filled creek that meanders through the southside.

A committee whittled the names to five. Four ranged from bland (Bull Frogs, Boxers, Barracudas—these last seldom found in the Tonawanda) to inane (Thunderbats). The fifth was the superb and indigenous "Muckdogs."

Muck is the fertile black soil that made Elba, the town bordering Batavia to the north, the "Onion Capital of the World." Given that the sports-marketing possibilities of bulbous plants are limited, muck seemed the more promising hook. What Batavia Muckdogs lacked in euphony it made up for in punch, promising to be as memorable as the Toledo Mud Hens or the Lansing Lugnuts.

Voters chose from among the five finalists, and a winner was selected under circumstances even murkier than those surrounding the 1948 count from Box 13 in Jim Wells County, Texas. In August 1997, the *Daily News* reported that the ball club had settled on a new mascot: a muck-spattered cur baring his fangs, a terror to everyone but personal injury lawyers. Batavia met the Muckdogs.

The name set off the fiercest local controversy since St. Joe's gave the philanthropic madam Edna Gruber a Catholic burial. For the next three months, the *Daily News* was filled with angry letters denouncing the poor muckdog as an undignified symbol.

Dr. Roth, club president, sought to placate the hostiles with a charming little fable, published in the indispensable *Daily News*. It told the tale of a family that left a "big, cold, and unfriendly" city for the bounteous blessings of the Genesee County, with its "bird watchers" and "real Indian reservation." Dick and Jane, the children of this family in the new Eden, found the dog of their dreams at the town's shelter, filling out "all the necessary paperwork that has to be done even in Genesee County." As for the dog's provenance, "He had some dark, rich dirt on his feet and fur, so it seemed as though he had come from the Muck. Jane then wanted to know what the Muck was. She learned it was a special area known throughout the country as the place where premium vegetables like onions and potatoes were grown. . . . Dick and Jane exclaimed, 'Now we know what to call him. He is going to be our Muckdog, our special friend forever!' "

The feral beast was all wagging tail and slathering tongue around the children, and they all lived happily ever after.

Incredibly, this nativity tale failed to quell the rebellion. A boycott was announced by pious folk. These rebels were convinced that the local guttersnipes would come up with creative rhymes for "Muckdogs." Even here, the fault line split along a quasi-ethnic divide. What we might call the "Fuckdog faction" was dominated by those whose family names end with a vowel. Their prolific ringleader was Carol Grasso, who is among the angels behind Crossroads House, which does Mother Teresa–like work in ministering to the dying.

"God help us if our team has a bad year next season," Grasso wrote in her first letter to the *Daily News*. "Every sign in town that has 'Muckdogs' on it surely will be vandalized. I hope not! But you know how kids can be. Speaking of kids, how about all the little kids who have speech problems[?]"

Out-localizing even a provincial like me, Grasso objected to the adoption of a name rooted five miles outside of Batavia. "The muck lands are in Elba, not Batavia. I don't ever remember seeing any muckers at any of the games I was at."

Après Grasso, the deluge. Kathy Chimino pointed out, "It doesn't take a genius to change the *M* to another letter of the alphabet and get a whole new meaning to the name." Dominic Tiberio asked if the Muckdog fanciers were "the people who thought it was a good idea to knock down the buildings on Main Street and ruin the culture of this city in the name of Urban Renewal?" Sue Fleming wrote, "Get someone with a few beers in them or the team has a bad game and we all hate to hear what they're called!"

Ralph "Bud" Williams, the genial retired printer whose campaign had earlier convinced the ball club to remove the Marlboro advertisement in right field, proposed that "the new name should be the Batavia Sniffenpoopers." Vern Kelly imagined the Muckdog "reeking of onions," disposing of former mascot Chipper the Clipper after "a few seconds of violent shaking and snarling."

Defenders of the much-reviled Muckdog chastised the boycotters as "city slickers" who "put down the muckers of Elba" because they "do not want to be associated with farmers." The coiner of Muckdog, a young father named Jay Moran, finally shamed the Fuckdogs into silence. Moran testified that he and his wife settled upon Muckdog as a name that was "quirky, offer[ed] some local flavor, and basically beg[ged] the question, 'What the heck is that?' " He apologized for any offense the name had given, though he did wonder if similar objections were ever lodged against the Trojans, given its prophylactic association. Moran concluded, "We thought it was a fun name for a fun enterprise, Batavia baseball. . . . I only know that next summer my family will attend games and cheer for our team. That's what fans do. I only hope that others will do the same."

Come June, the boycott fizzled—attendance for the Muckdogs was slightly higher than it was for the Clippers and the Trojans, 1,000 a game, more on Fourth of July Fireworks Night, less on chilly late August evenings. Profane rhymesters never materialized, and the beleaguered hound emerged as a veritable St. Bernard of the diamond.

In its first year as the Muckdogs, the team made $80,000 in merchandise sales, or about $75,000 more than in previous years. Little League teams from Georgia, Texas, Colorado, and Maryland wear Muckdog togs; so do softball teams from the onion-less otherlands. Freddie Prinze Jr. wore a Muckdogs jersey in *Summer Catch*, a film not directed by Jean Cocteau.

The Muckdog helped keep Batavia out of the red-ink sea. But baseball is an unsentimental business, and absent a population explosion, the future of history-steeped but yuppie-shy baseball cities is hazy. Batavia is one of the smallest markets in all of professional baseball, though we are only the second-smallest in the NYP League. Year in and year out, we rank at or near the bottom of the league in attendance.

As a condition of New York State's subsidy to renovate Dwyer, our franchise is guaranteed through 2006, and we retain at least a fighting chance to survive beyond that. For Batavia is a community-owned club—government-owned, as my libertarian friends would say—and thus not hostage to the whims or avarice of an individual or corporate owner. The team belongs to the city and is administered by the nonprofit Batavia Regional Recreation Corporation. ("Recreation" sounded broader, more *inclusive*, than "Baseball.") The Muckdogs, unlike, say, the Cleveland Browns, can't be sold like a '73 Camaro, at least not unless a majority of the city council wants to raise some quick cash. I suppose this is socialism, and my vote is

usually for liberty. But in the umpire's call of "Batter up!" the cog-
nitive dissonance vanishes.

No matter the paper guarantees, we had best store memories while
we can. Each summer's end is the time for melancholy reflections.
Actually, no season is safe from my melancholy reflecting, but be
that as it may, the depressing and pointless Labor Day holiday means
the end of Batavia baseball for another year, as the Muckdogs scatter
to the baseball winds (which tend to run in southerly and increasingly
Dominican directions).

At the last game of the year, Dennis Bowler, a fifty-seven-year-
old bachelor farmer and member in good standing of the third-base
bleacher gang, presents my daughter with a baseball bat on which
he has engraved *Gretel* while tending the roadside stand at which he
sells corn from his twenty acres. She is thrilled, he is gratified, I am
touched beyond words.

Another season comes to a close, and in the fall-whispering chill
of the final innings of the season, I hear the echoes of sixty years:
the long-dead drunkards' slurred maledictions against the blind
umps, the "Can I have your autograph, please?" entreaties of boys
become men. August is done.

◻ ◻ ◻

And after the last out . . .

Larry Roth, born in 1917, grew up a farmboy from nearby Stafford.
The town, Genesee County's WASP nest, was settled by families from
Devonshire, but Devon sounded too much like a teenage boy, so they
called it Stafford, the family name of the Duke of Devonshire.

Educated at Batavia High School, Larry Roth went on to Hobart
College in Geneva. There he met Catherine Kirchner, a strong-willed
and rectitudinous Long Island girl studying at Hobart's sister college,
William Smith. They fell in love, and she became Catherine Roth.

Larry Roth the yokel trombonist became Dr. Roth at the Yale
Medical School. After wartime military service, he and Catherine

settled in Batavia. He was a gynecologist and the director of the medical staff at Genesee Memorial, one of Batavia's two hospitals. (The other, St. Jerome, was founded in 1917 by Catholics unhappy with the Protestant Lady Bountifuls who guided Genesee Memorial.)

Catherine, whom a college newspaper called "modest and unassuming" and who was never thereafter associated with either word, plunged into the usual beneficent works of a doctor's wife in a prefeminist small town.

When, in the mid-1960s, the city fathers signed the pact with the devil known as urban renewal, Catherine became the most visible preservationist in Batavia, doing the Lord's work in vain.

Catherine—the outsider, the interloper, the "goddam busybody," as Ray Doody called her—spoke for the shades of Batavia's past, but the democracy of the dead was no match for Mammon. We got renewed, but good.

And still, Catherine kept at it, addressing the city fathers in a lofty old pre-sprawl Long Island accent and becoming, at once, the most respected and most detested woman in the city. She ran for city council, won, and battled council president Benny Potrzebowksi, proprietor of the working-man's bar called Kelly's Holland Inn ("City Council South," in Catherine's tart phrase), in a conflict dense with ethno-cultural-religious significance. (Only in Batavia could a Polack own an Irishman's bar named for the Dutch.)

From her split-level ranch house on the doctors' end of East Avenue, Catherine edited a magnificent coffee-table book, *The Architectural Heritage of Genesee County*, 300 pages of photographs taken before the vinyl-siding salesmen moved in. She is a great woman, capable of interrupting a program on women's rights at the Wednesday Study Club by announcing, "It's noon, and I have to go home to make lunch for Lah-ree."

In retirement, Dr. Roth, or Lah-ree, seems a languidly ovoid octogenarian. Then you realize that the Muckdogs, Genesee Memorial Hospital, the Batavia Concert Band, and the Genesee Symphony Orchestra have all rested, in varying degrees, upon his shoulders.

He followed his wife into the controversialist's role when he became the ringleader of the movement, ultimately successful, to prevent St. Jerome from absorbing Genesee Memorial. Larry, who before the hospital bloodbath hadn't an enemy in the world, carried a heavy cross.

As Sinclair Lewis, Gopher Prairie's most loving if unloved son, understood, a resentment of success lurks just beneath the surface of every small town. The successful draw out the venom when they begin their letters to the editor of the *Daily News* with "Listen up!" as Dr. Roth was wont to do. When south-side Democrats on the city council balked at spending tax dollars on the Dwyer Stadium renovation, Dr. Roth exhorted them "to play ball and to be winners." This innocent locution was bound to be misconstrued by Jackson Street Italians who don't live in Rothian split-levels and whose clock-punching paychecks from our increasingly union-less factories do not make them "winners" according to the rules handed down from on high.

Dr. Roth was a great man, but his people were outnumbered in the new Batavia, so he was headed for a great fall.

A month after the 2000 season's end, at about the time that my melancholy reflections ripen into morose cogitations, much to my surprise, and the surprise of the beheaded himself, a bloodless coup was executed. I heard it first from Catherine.

"They got rid of Lah-ree," she announced over the phone in her best the-peasants-are-revolting declaration.

"Whaddaya mean?" I stammered, my usual eloquent self.

"The baaawd voted him out. Dennis Dwy-uh is the new president."

Dennis is the grandson of Ed Dwyer, eponym of the ballpark, the compact merchant Irishman with the white brush cut who in my mind's eye is forever heckling the twenty-one-year-old umpire behind the plate. (I have a photo of my dad and Pinky Dwyer, Ed's son and Dennis's father, grinning in rascally complicity, dressed in their Notre Dame baseball uniforms, sitting on the bench. They had been suspended for an infraction whose exact nature Dad has never ventured to make clear.)

The well-liked Dennis is in his late thirties; he runs Thomas & Dwyer, the family shoestore next to C. L. Carr's on the brick block that is the last redoubt of the old Batavia, calibrating insteps and casting a wary eye just outside the city limits, where Foot Locker, Payless, and the soleful but soulless chains mass in corporate phalanx. Dennis was a Comet—I identify all my male coevals by the minor or Little League teams on which they played—and not much of a catcher. But in adulthood he is a backstop of the rising Chamber of Commerce generation.

"He's a Democrat, you know," sighs Catherine, not bothering to add the obvious addendum that the Dwyers, whose branches often extend for eight children or more, are Catholic. (As a boy I thought of them as the Kennedys of Batavia—the girls were pretty, freckled colleens; two were killed in tragic automobile accidents.) I am also Catholic and Democrat, but Catherine looks beyond these disabilities.

"You know what they-ah doing? They-ah getting rid of all the Republicans." This is a reference to the perpetual war of Catholic and Protestant, Democrat and Republican, south side and north, which for the nonce is leaning toward the plebe side.

"Well, I'm sorry they did it," I say, honestly. "I can't believe it has anything to do with Democrats and Republicans, though." I think the board members just thought Larry was too old, though I don't say this to Catherine.

The vote, I learn, was twelve to nine in favor of Dennis. The balloting was done in secret. I had not been told of the meeting beforehand, even though that night I was to be elected a new board member. I tell Catherine that although I respect Dennis, had I been there I'd have voted for Doc Roth, as I would have, traitor to my class or no.

But ah, the Brutus in this play, the Muckdogs director who nominated Dennis Dwyer, takes me aback. It was Ricky, the baseball savant and indispensable Batavian.

I see Ricky two weeks later at the Batavia Rotary Club's annual show, which is staged in the Blind School auditorium on a November night. The talented director, Linda Blanchet, wife of a dentist and head of the Genesee-Orleans Arts Council, has broken with the long skein of *My Fair Lady*s and *Oklahoma!*s and *Music Man*s and is serving us *Side by Side by Sondheim*. It is, shall we say, an imperfect match of audience and material. The narrator, kindly Mr. Hay, conductor of the Batavia Blue Devils Marching Band, cracks double entendres to a roomful of titters and throat clearings. When he explains the difference between disappointment and despair—disappointment is the first time you realize you can't do it twice in a night, and despair is the second time you realize you can't do it once—I smile wanly and sink in my seat. Oh, Mr. Hay!

The crowd thins at intermission—next year my money's on *Hello, Dolly*—but we stick it out, knowing that Wanda would want us to.

The show ends, the crowd files out, not humming "Send in the Clowns," and I spot Ricky in the lobby. I ask him what happened. "I don't know," he spits in his rapid fire, accelerated, perhaps, by guilt. "Doc said in August he dinno if he wannid to do it anymore. I thought he wannid to retire. I dinno."

And he walks away.

I have known Ricky since I was twelve. He is guileless, thoroughly decent, and he is no fool. Nor is he a cat's paw.

Ricky, the smartest kid ever assigned to the slow class, Ricky of falling-down Pringle Park, perennial laughingstock team of the park baseball league, Ricky upon whose face is written "south-side working class," made the motion that brought down the most influential and distinguished physician in Batavia.

Conceding every nit and complication, that smells like democracy to me.

CHAPTER FOUR

The Blessed Spirit Joins the Rotary (Political Batavia)

In Batavia, the artists are Republicans. The rosary bead–counting ladies baking St. Joseph's bread and signing "Respect Life" petitions in the narthex of St. Anthony's are the Democrats. Watercolorist John Hodgins, who delights in splashy oranges and yellows, was a GOP fixture on the city council and now sits on the county legislature. There is no more devoted party man and deprecator of Democrats than pencil sketch artist Don Carmichael. Our late friend Virginia Carr Mumford, a touring pianist and accomplished portraitist, sent money to Oliver North and the rest of the scam artists of Northern Virginia Conservatism, Inc. That is, until her son Peter took to intercepting the purloining letters.

The undisputed leader of Batavia Republicans is the orthodontist Dr. Roger, recently retired Rear Admiral in the U.S. Navy's Dental Reserve Corps. Dr. Roger once presided over the Genesee County legislature with a pomp not always warranted by circumstance: one imagined that he would not have objected to a few bars of "Hail to the Chief," at least every now and then. He resigned that position to take a part-time post with Governor George Pataki—the Hungarian nonentity who regularly stabs rural Yorkers in the back because he knows that every four years the Democrats will nominate a rebarbative Noo Yaawka who will not even bother to hide his contempt for us simple people of the hills and vales.

For years, Dr. Roger has officiated at our county's military-related events, such as the unveiling of a plaque to our Civil War hero, Charles Rand. Dr. Roger is, after all, the highest-ranking military officer in these parts, an admiral in our landlocked duchy. During the Gulf War, the Admiral pontificated in the *Daily News* on matters martial—and I don't mean the war on plaque. He was fond of recalling the epic occasion on which he met General Colin Powell. Admiral to General, as it were.

He is our Clausewitz, our Patton. Our fitter of removable bite plates.

We did not always strive merely to bask in Colin Powell's shadow. Batavia's moment in the national political sun, or at least its penumbra, came in the fall of 1826. In that epochal autumn, the abduction and probable murder of an itinerant stonemason and garrulous drunk named Captain William Morgan set off the frenzy of anti-Masonry. This was not an aversion to bricklaying but rather the demonization of the fraternal organization descended from medieval guilds.

Masonry was the "craft" to its initiates—and little short of witchcraft to the uninitiated.

Anti-Masonry strikes the modern ear as an absurdity, on the order of anti-Rotarianism. For land's sake, what do the Masons *do*, other than sponsor Little League teams and leer at the wives of the Knights of Columbus? Yet when lightning struck in 1826, this strange sentiment coalesced into what historian John B. McMaster called "the most remarkable" political party in U.S. history: the Anti-Masons.

Yes, it happened here. Shudder.

I have a copy of an idiosyncratic "History of Masonry in Batavia" delivered in 1942 to the Batavia Lodge #475, Free and Accepted Masons, by William H. Coon. This polymathic Batavia attorney taught children flute and saxophone and enjoyed speechifying on "the trial of Christ from a legal point of view."

Old Judge Coon, as my dad and the boys used to call him, lived in a fittingly substantial home at the corner of North and State Streets, a few strides from what is now the hip-hop Batavia of lower State. Dad still calls it the Coon house.

Which brings to mind a Sunday morning at Perkins when Dad was chaffing with Carm Vega, the undisputed "best waitress in town." Carm, a vivacious ex-BHS cheerleader, is also a member of one of Batavia's larger black families. (Her dream is to move with her children to Norway. She has visited Oslo and warns us that one day she will be gone, expatriated to the land of Liv Ullman and televised cross-country skiing.) Besides waitressing, Carm cleans thirty-six homes either weekly or biweekly, which gives her workweeks of seven 14-hour days. The Judge's old place is among the thirty-six.

"I saw you down at the Coon house," Dad said to Carm that Sunday morn, prompting one of the great double takes in the history of Batavia race relations.

And now back to the Masons. According to Judge Coon's history, the first Batavia lodge was formed in May 1810. Coon notes that Governor DeWitt Clinton, Most Worshipful Grand Master, approved the lodge's petition. By 1826, the Batavia Lodge #433 consisted of sixty active members, of which only two, according to Coon, ever renounced the craft. In for a penny, in for a pound, I guess. And in for a corpse.

The corpse bore the name of William Morgan. At the time of his death, he was fifty-two, "a Southerner," notes Coon, who had fought under the Mason Andy Jackson at the Battle of New Orleans. Shiftless, footloose, quarrelsome, and bibulous, he wound up in these parts and "bamboozled" the nearby Le Roy chapter of the Masons into exalting him to a Royal Arch Mason in 1825.

Morgan was no-account white trash, always nursing a grievance. But unlike most members of the craft, William Morgan really was a stonemason. His first job was the Jackson Street residence later known as the Genesee Hotel, which was, in best Batavia tradition, razed in the mid-twentieth century. By 1826, Morgan was a resident of Batavia. He applied to join the Batavia Masonic lodge and was rejected. Then the world changed.

Enraged at this blackballing, Morgan engaged David C. Miller, publisher of the Batavia *Republican Advocate*, to publish *Illustrations of Freemasonry*, in which were revealed the oaths and pledges and other arcana of this secret society.

"One rap calls the Lodge to order," begins Morgan's exposé, a meticulous description of the rituals of Freemasonry, spiced with hints of erotic masochism (naked male breasts impaled with the point of a compass) and lurid adolescent fantasies of punishment. (The Mason apostate agrees "to have my throat cut across, my tongue torn out by the roots and my body buried in the rough sands of the sea at low water-mark.")

While *Illustrations of Freemasonry* was in the antebellum equivalent of galleys, the Masons caught wind of its forthcoming publication. Morgan was arrested on the trumped-up charge of stealing a hat, for which dastardly crime he was locked in jail. Daredevil Masons kidnapped him from his cell and administered their own rough justice. They drowned Morgan in the Niagara River—or at least that is the belief of all non-Masons, for the body never washed ashore, and ne'er more was Morgan seen. (To this day, loyal Masons insist that the sot skulked off to Canada and drank himself into old age.)

Overnight, William Morgan, town drunk, became Captain Morgan, martyr. Morgan's disappearance was desultorily investigated by a legal-political structure rife with Masons, including Governor DeWitt Clinton. Grand juries handed down more than fifty indictments of implicated Masons in the Morgan case, but punishments were lenient—a few days here and there, nothing to match being buried at low tide or even a good nipple-pricking. The fix was in, or so it seemed to the good non-Masonic farmers and mechanics of western New York. The region was already on the verge of a great and fiery religious revival: Morgan's murder lit the match, and the tinderbox blew.

Anti-Masons held raucous caucuses that resembled revival meetings. Animated by the "blessed spirit," they sang lustily:

The Freemen bring the monster,
Before the public place it,
  And though it scowl
  With phiz most foul,
Will Anti-Masons face it.

How absolutely baffling it must have been for your typical Mason—a well-to-do merchant, a prosperous and respected Protestant man of the town—to wake one morning and find himself vituperated as a Princeling of Darkness! Decades after the firestorm, one elderly New York Mason recalled the cataclysm: "Masons were excluded from a participation in the Holy Communion; their names were thrown out of the jury box; and at the social gatherings of the grave matrons of the neighborhood, resolutions were . . . passed forbidding their daughters from keeping company with a Mason."

The fury concretized into an Anti-Masonic Party, which in its newborn purity rested on a single plank: to bar Masons from political office, juries, indeed all of public life.

In 1827, the Anti-Masons won fifteen seats in the New York Assembly. In 1828, the party's gubernatorial candidate, the true believer Solomon Southwick, whose habit it was to base major decisions on the flip of a coin, won 12 percent of the vote, sweeping the scorched counties of Genesee, Wyoming, Orleans, and three others.

By 1831, Anti-Masons held the governorship of Vermont and had come within 8,000 votes of capturing the same office in New York. Damning secret societies became all the rage: John Quincy Adams, trawling for Anti-Masonic votes in his presidential campaign of 1828, offered to expose the treacheries of Phi Beta Kappa.

Then the blessed spirit up and died. A host of career politicians descended upon anti-Masonry. Men who would found the Whig and Republican Parties—William Seward, Thurlow Weed, Millard Fillmore, Horace Greeley—cut their eyeteeth in the party. Recognizing the limitations of the language of the Antichrist, this cadre of tailored young lawyers ousted the red-hots and committed the party to the Henry Clay program of high tariffs, a national bank, canals and other internal improvements, and sundry matters unrelated to the Beast with Seven Heads.

In 1832, the denatured Anti-Masons nominated an unrepentant ex-Mason, former Attorney General William Wirt, to run for president against Masons Andrew Jackson and Henry Clay. Wirt carried only Vermont, and the party was finished. The smooth alchemists Weed and Seward mixed the Anti-Masonic dross with Henry Clay's National Republicans to create the Whigs.

Thus did the first third party in American politics become the first third party to be sold out by its leaders. By 1833, the Anti-Masons had vanished as thoroughly as snow from an October squall.

And what of Masonry? The order was decimated in the Northeast. In 1825, the Masons counted 480 lodges and 20,000 members in New York; a decade later, they numbered fewer than 50 lodges with 3,000 adherents, barely enough to beat the Odd Fellows at a summer picnic tug of war.

However tempting it is for us sophisticates to sneer at the Anti-Masons' "conspiracy theories," the Masonic influence was unquestionably pervasive, as indicated in this 1825 address by a Masonic orator: "What is masonry now? It is powerful. It comprises men of rank, wealth, office, and talent, in power and out of power . . . active men, united together, and capable of being directed by the efforts of others, so as to have the force of concert throughout the civilized world." Add a Rockefeller and you've got the Council on Foreign Relations.

They were mighty, they were legion, and they were everywhere. Grand Masters of New York Masonry had included Governor Clinton, Vice President (under James Monroe) Daniel Tompkins, and such patroons as Livingstons and Van Rensselaers. George Washington, Benjamin Franklin, Lafayette, and numerous Founders had been Masons, as were Capitol architect Benjamin Latrobe and Surveyor General Andrew Ellicott (brother of the churlish Joseph, founder of Batavia). Masonic architects and sculptors, aided by Masonic politicians, adorned Washington's public buildings with the celestial and geometric symbols of Masonry. There are twenty-three important zodiacs in Washington, far more than one finds in such sublunary burgs as London and New York City.

So is it any wonder that one Anti-Mason wrote Weed, "Charge it with almost any thing and it can be proved. There are few things it is not guilty of"—including sodomizing goats, rumor had it.

As lodge brothers of the Enlightenment, Masons were also anti-Catholic. The feeling was mutual: only in 1982 did the R.C. Church drop its ban on Masonic membership. But in the 1820s, wafer-worshippers were not yet a significant presence in Batavia. St. Joseph's, Batavia's first Catholic church, was not founded until 1849, by which time Masonry was humbled and diminished.

The last rites—whether for Masonry or anti-Masonry it is not clear—were held half a century later, on September 13, 1882, when two hundred pious delegates of the Illinois-based National Christian Association Opposed to Secret Societies met in Batavia and dedicated a 37-feet-high, 40-ton marble cenotaph to Captain William Morgan.

"The people of this village generally ridicule the idea of erecting the monument at this late date," commented the *New York Times*. But two Batavia old-timers, Judge Moses Taggert and Miss Sarah Stevens, wowed the crowd with glory-days reminiscences of 1826. For some years afterward, local Masons kept a vigilant eye on the Morgan monument, or so claim the brethren, to guard against vandalism that surely would have been blamed on the craft.

The cenotaph still stands, undefaced. Walk through the gates of the Old Batavia Cemetery, across the street from the abandoned Massey-Harris plant on Harvester Avenue. Pass the Hepzibahs and

Phineases of a distant age, and at the southwest corner of our pioneer necropolis Captain Morgan strains like Tantalus, mere yards from the beery conviviality of Uncle Tony's Pizzeria. "The bane of our civil institutions is to be found in Masonry, already powerful and becoming more so," reads the weathered inscription. "I owe to my country an exposure of its dangers."

The dedication says:

SACRED TO THE MEMORY OF

WILLIAM MORGAN

A Native of Virginia,
A Capt. in the War of 1812,
A Respectable Citizen of
Batavia, and a Martyr
To the Freedom of Writing
Printing and Speaking the
Truth. He was abducted
From near this spot in the
Year 1826, By FreeMasons
And Murdered for revealing
The Secrets of their Order.

Erected by Volunteer
Contributions from over
2000 Persons residing in
Canada, Ontario,
And twenty-six of the
United States
And Territories.

Batavia Lodge #475 (unlucky #433 dissolved in the Morgan moment) is down to about a dozen members. It no longer even sponsors the Masonic Comets of the Batavia Boys' Minor League. And yet I daren't scoff, for I drive past mute Captain Morgan all the time—and in Batavia, we know better than to get on the wrong side of the Masons.

If anti-Masonry represents the feverish side of the Batavia imagination (if I may be grandiose), its Rotarian mundaneness is embodied by Dean Richmond, our industrial magnate, nonrepellent division. Richmond is the titan whose Greek Revival mansion was converted into the Edna Gruber–subsidized Children's Home and then demolished to make a parking lot by the learned solons of the Batavia Board of Education.

I must tread carefully here. The agreed-upon facts are these: the Board of Education purchased the Children's Home in 1966, the centenary of Dean Richmond's death, for $75,000. Its nefarious plan was to demolish it and build an annex to the Richmond Library, with its red sandstone gargoyles, which Dean's widow had built in 1889 as a memorial to Dean Jr.

Voters rejected the annex in a referendum, whereupon the Board, claiming that it would cost $105,000 to restore the mansion and $5,000 to tear it down, let loose wrecking ball upon pillar.

The ruins became the St. Joseph's parking lot. The library's cement-slab annex was later built in the popular late twentieth-century minimum security prison style.

"You can't blame that one on the Catholics," I prod Catherine Roth: hell, the Board president was no other than Herb Brenner, a Jewish jeweler, whose motto was "It's always okay to owe Herb Brenner." (But not for too long, wise Batavians used to add.)

Catherine, however, insists that the incense burners are the real villains. She says that Monsignor Schwartz coveted the prime parking space and put out the word that his coreligionists were to act so as to encourage demolition. I scoff at her unified field theory of Catholic iniquity even as I suspect its truth. In Batavia, we know about conspiracies.

❏ ❏ ❏

Stout and grumpy in portrait, Dean Richmond "was bluff and he was brusque," according to the railroad historian Edward Hungerford. But then, he was born in Vermont, and it can be difficult to leave an idealized picture postcard for a real place. The longtime vice president of the New York Central Railroad, Richmond ascended to the presidency in 1864. His death two years later, at age sixty-six, paved the way for that thieving bastard (and ancestor of the anorexic ghoul Gloria) Cornelius Vanderbilt to steal the line.

Richmond's wretched penmanship has kept biographers at bay. His surviving correspondence is simply unreadable. In any event, he was neither flat-out rogue nor model of probity: "Richmond was not generally regarded as perfidious," is the restrained judgment of one ethicist. The surviving anecdotes fall this side of endearing.

Local historian Bill Brown relates: "Once the Central's chief executive forgot to reserve a drawing room chair and had to sit in an ordinary coach. A passenger behind him objected when the burly Richmond opened a window. The man reached around him and closed it. Richmond opened it. The man again shut it. Richmond then took his cane and smashed the window, bellowing, 'Now close it if you can.' " Charming.

Richmond was the Democratic State Chairman from 1857 to 1866. He was a Stephen Douglas man in 1860, though his favorite son was Horatio Seymour. As New York governor, Seymour would prove among the most courageous and principled critics of Father Lincoln's immense abridgements of American liberties: conscription, the suspension of habeas corpus, the jailing of dissenters and closing of newspapers, the exiling of Ohio Democrat Clement Vallandigham, and other tyrannical acts that somehow never make it into the Social Studies syllabus.

Richmond steered a middle course during the war. He was not a treasonably antiwar patriot like Vallandigham, nor did he bolt the Democracy for preferment and power on the Republican side. He was neither full-throated warmonger nor craven pro-slavery dough-face: Montgomery Blair, Lincoln's Postmaster General, named Dean Richmond the man most responsible for the adoption of the anti-slavery Thirteenth Amendment, for Richmond acted behind the scenes to sway the potent New York congressional delegation.

After the war, Richmond vainly promoted a "National Union Party" of safe, sane, sensible men of North and South, but it came a cropper upon his death at the Gramercy Park home of Samuel Tilden, the "Great Forecloser" as he was known to the hard-pressed mort-gagees of New York City.

We may hope that our Dean was consoled in those final days by what was reputed to be Tilden's Alexandria-sized library of pornog-raphy. Whether Tilden would have moved his stash of Gilded Age *Penthouses* into the White House had the Republicans not stolen the 1876 presidential election from him is a matter best left to historians of presidential erections.

Tilden's eulogy for Richmond contained this surprise: "It is my firm conviction that except for that refusal his nomination was entirely possible [in 1864] and his election extremely probable."

All that stood between Batavia and the Presidency was . . . Abra-ham Lincoln. And Batavia, you may be sure, would have gone solidly for Lincoln, as the prophet, or in this case the profiteer, is always without honor in his hometown. For even in death, our Democrat was snubbed: Batavia's finest hotel, the Eagle, was briefly renamed the Hotel Richmond, until protests forced a quick reversion to its appel-lation honoring the American bird of prey.

◻ ◻ ◻

Today I walk Richmond Avenue, its magnificent maples standing bough in bough, as if linked in arboreal defiance of the Niagara

Mohawk chainsaw. I visit the Richmond Memorial Library, never glancing at the portraits of various Richmonds, some productive and others consumptive, their progeny scattered to the gale-force American winds. Our first family—almost your First Family, too—remains entombed in its mausoleum, deader than the passenger train. I wish the mansion were still here, tenanted by an old Richmond maid or queer Richmond bachelor with whom I could take tea (even though I hate tea) and listen for ghosts. But the Board of Education fixed that all right.

Edmund Wilson, responding to his own question, "Do you remember the Civil War?" replied, "Oh, very well. I was a drummer boy at Gettysburg, one of the big battles. But later on I came to realize that the South ought to have been allowed to secede from the Union— that was the great issue for the North rather than slavery, you know— and I deserted and took refuge in upstate New York, which has always been rather disaffected. I became what is known as a Copperhead."

Rather disaffected—I like that. Wilson's heir, Gore Vidal of the Hudson Valley, is also a Copperhead, an antiwar northerner, as was one of Wilson's pet causes, the bigamist novelist Harold Frederic of Utica. Frederic produced an extraordinary novella (*The Copperhead*) which sympathetically depicts a Mohawk Valley farmer who opposes the War Between the States and pays for it with a burned barn. Chastened and shamed, his remorseful neighbors help him rebuild.

So if we don't live on Copperhead Road, we at least have a few snakes in the woodpile. As a Jeffersonian democrat with antiwar convictions and abolitionist sympathies myself, I am attracted less to Dean Richmond, bless his avaricious heart, than to the Bunny Wilsons and Gore Vidals, of whom I have found a single anonymous Batavia representative: my dad picked me up a November 23, 1861, issue of the Batavia *Spirit of the Times*, which contains the results of the November 5, 1861, canvas. And there, in the write-ins in the race for State Senate, we find one vote for "Jeff. Davis." God bless the iconoclast. Of thee I sing. But should I? If the archetypal Batavian voted Lincoln, Garfield, McKinley, Hoover, Ike, and so on down the Wall Street line, shouldn't I have *voted* for the Bushes instead of pissing in them?

My family had hoped that upon graduating from college I would take the civil service test and become a mailman. Steady government work, good union wages. I had always liked getting mail, and 'tis better to give than to receive. But no, I had ambitions political. Republicans had obliterated my city so I was a Democrat, albeit a Mugwump reformist.

I cringe to recall that in 1980, as a college senior, I was flukishly nominated as a presidential elector on the John Anderson ticket. That hoar-headed pile of piety was running at 25 percent in New York in the spring of '80, so while shooting hoops in my driveway, I day-dreamed that I, Elector, held the key to the White House. As I clanged ten-foot jumpers off the back rim I primly rejected the pro-ferred whores sent to my suite by the Carter and Reagan camps. Oh, I oozed republican virtue.

You may recall that in May of 1981 I went to work for the poor man's Mugwump, Senator Pat Moynihan. He shall ever occupy a lukewarm place in my heart for blistering me as a "fucking idiot" as we ran to catch the Capitol subway for a meeting that I had judi-ciously neglected to pencil in on his schedule somewhere between naps.

Of Pat—or "Senator," as we browbeaten intimates of the ever-changing staff called him—I shall have little to say other than that he was the only statewide Democrat in recent memory who under-stood Upstate. He and his wife, Liz, owned a farmhouse in Pindars Corners, near Oneonta, which permitted him to call himself the Sen-ate's only dairy farmer. I can't really see Pat Moynihan squat on a stable stool, squeezing the last drop from Bessie's teats, but then I've a dash of the typewriter agrarian in me, too, to borrow Mencken's dismissive phrase, so we'll grant Moynihan his bovine presumptions. They are no more far-fetched than his claim to have risen out of Hell's Kitchen—which Ed Koch waggishly corrected to "Hell's Condominium."

Moynihan was capable of speaking truths: the CIA ought to be abolished; we should bring our troops home from Europe; the problems of urban American blacks are intractable with current rates of family deformation. Alas, he was incapable of acting on them. He was a spearless leader, the cowardly lion of post-liberal Democrats. Nevertheless, he could be mordantly wise, as witness his remark to a reporter when driving through the decimated downtown of Auburn, New York: "In the 1950s, with a progressive government and newspaper, you got into urban renewal and destroyed everything of value in your town. If you'd had a reactionary newspaper, and a grumpy mayor, you might still have it."

That is worth a "fucking idiot" or two.

Moynihan's favorite member of Congress, himself excepted, was Batavia's sole twentieth-century contribution to the national polity. He was, by my lights, the most eminent political figure we have ever produced: Barber B. Conable Jr.

Richard Fenno, the foremost congressional scholar of his generation, called him "the best of the breed." Conable consistently won the *Washingtonian* magazine poll of his colleagues as the most respected member of the House of Representatives. Woodward and Bernstein gushed that "he was regarded by his colleagues as almost puritanical in his standards of personal and political conduct, a man of unquestioned integrity." Sighed George Will, "There never has been a better congressman."

He served twenty years in Congress, most prominently as the ranking Republican on the House Ways and Means Committee, where he shone alongside such examples of mediocrity and/or turpitude as Chairmen Wilbur Mills, Al Ullman, and Dan Rostenkowski. Upon his retirement in 1985 he went on to be president of the World Bank. All of which equips Mr. Conable with the necessary fiduciary skills to man the cashbox at the Holland Purchase Historical Society's annual yard sale.

American politicians get all mushy over the virtues of the home folks—none finer, they say. But how many ever go back to live among them? When James Madison wrote that congressmen "must descend to the level from which they are raised," he had Barber Conable in mind. For if his career was exemplary, his retirement has been even more so; he is that exceedingly rare example of a man sent forth from a people who returns to them as both elder and neighbor.

Barber and his wife, Charlotte, live in a circa 1830 hybrid Federal–Greek Revival home on Main Street in Alexander, five miles south of Batavia on Route 98. (Alexander is a town of barely one thousand souls that also produced John Gardner and our martial orthodontist Dr. Roger.)

Conable moved seamlessly, un-self-consciously, between two worlds. Even in retirement, one day he would be in Washington, chairing the executive committee of the Smithsonian Institution's Board of Regents, and the next night he and Charlotte were in Batavia, sitting around a Formica-top table in the Holland Land Office Museum and discussing with other directors of the Holland Purchase Historical Society (including me) how much we should spend on toner for the Xerox machine. He was until very recently chairman of the National Committee on U.S.–China Relations; he is also a trustee of the Alexander Village Cemetery, his future home.

Conable is a first among equals in our local organizations. People are aware of his eminence, and respectful, but there is no tugging on forelocks or kissing of his ring. No man is ever really eminent at home, where they remember you when you were a runny-nosed kid or the struggling young lawyer with the funny name.

Besides, it's hard to be awestruck over someone who is ubiquitous. Conable does not play lord of the manor, graciously receiving visitors who come to pay him homage. He comes to us: Conable averages about a speech a month on local topics to local audiences. Unpaid, naturally—the assumption is that anyone who ran something called

the World Bank must be loaded—these are marvels of extempora-
neity. Conable delivers witty, learned, and discursive talks on our
Indians, our pioneers, our presidents (Millard Fillmore and Grover
Cleveland), our philanthropists and founders and scoundrels.

Some day, regional patriots will give talks about the legendary
Barber Conable, and thus will the circle be unbroken. (Millard
Fillmore, whose name has become a presidential punchline in
search of a joke, is something of a model for Conable, at least in
retirement. The ex-president moved home to become the "First Citizen of Buffalo," where he founded the city's Historical Society and
read Shakespeare to lift the souls of the toiling hands in a shoe
factory.)

Conable is simply part of the community: a revered elder, to be
sure, but one so well circulated as to be part of our currency. He is
auctioneer for local benefits; he seems always to be giving the keynote
address whenever one of our towns has its 175th anniversary; by long
tradition, he reads the Declaration of Independence on July 4th at
the Genesee Country Village (our Williamsburg, without the hidden
slaves), and he does so with such vehemence that "it makes you want
to strangle George III," as one museum aide says. He sups on Methodist chicken breast at our monthly historical society meetings, at
which he typically descants on such arcana as how his town's namesake, State Senator Alexander Rhea, bribed Aaron Burr to convince
the New York legislature to create our county of Genesee in 1802.
(Rhea the corrupt sleeps in the same Alexander Village Cemetery
overseen by Conable the Righteous.)

Most important of all, the Conables' three daughters all live within
ten miles of Alexander: a striking display of filial and regional affec-
tion by children who were raised part hick, part suburban Washington, and who have made the superbly sensible—if atypical—choice
of rural Upstate New York over Chevy Chase.

The Conable den is plastered not with yellowing photos of for-
gettable pols ("Here I am shaking Milton Shapp's hand," says the

pathetico) but with Indian artifacts: tomahawks and images of Red Jacket, Cornplanter, Handsome Lake—the natural leaders of the previous inhabitants of these parts.

"Those arrowheads on that plaque my mother sewed on cardboard for me when I was twelve years old," Conable says. Paintings by regional artists—Lemuel Wiles, Noah North, Batavia's Roy Mason— adorn the living room, keeping an uneasy watch over Chinese and Moroccan knicknacks, the exotic booty hauled home by the Conables after their lustrum at the World Bank.

"Why did you retire to Alexander rather than stick around Washington?" I ask. "Because it's my home," he replies, an excellent answer, if not the usual one, else Bob Dole would be calling Bingo at the Russell Volunteer Fire Department and Bill Clinton would be humping harlots in Hope.

The last thing Barber Conable could have been is a lobbyist, which is the first thing he was asked to be upon leaving office in 1985. "There's nothing deader than a dead politician," he says. "I recall my friends Wilbur Mills and Al Ullman coming to lobby me after they had gone to their rewards one way or another, and I would duck into doorways to avoid them because they would be asking for things that I knew they didn't believe in. They were pure mercenaries.

"I could have stayed in Washington at six figures if I had wanted to. I considered it. But they wanted a stuffed exhibit and not a lawyer, and I didn't want to be a stuffed exhibit. They wanted to use my name and put me in the firm and give me a special 'of counsel' status. At the appropriate time the senior partner would push a button and I would come into the consultation he was having with his client and he'd say, 'You remember former Congressman Barber Conable, don't you? Remember the great role he played in Ways and Means?' That image frightened me."

So instead it was home to Alexander. Though he had never really left.

□ □ □

Barber Conable still makes the five-mile drive into Batavia every Saturday morning to meet for coffee and donuts and gossip at Genesee Hardware. This coffee klatsch—consisting of the hardware store owner, a banker, the YMCA director, and other community pillars: some wise, some bullshitters, several now dead—has met at 7:30 A.M. every Saturday since 1952.

"We called it 'coffee with the boys,' " says Conable. "Of course everybody there is over eighty years old. I am still 'Young Conable.' "

He kept his date for coffee with the boys even during his twenty years in Congress. "I made a serious effort to remain rooted," he says. But it is his continued membership in the club, long after its superannuated fixtures might do him political good, that suggests the strength of the tie that binds Conable to his homeplace. He did not go to Congress because he hired a slick advertising agency and beamed commercials into the loneliest dales, interrupting *The Beverly Hillbillies* and urging the yokels to vote for a man they'd never met. Conable came *from* the people, and to them he has returned; like the cream in the dairies of his Wyoming County birthplace, he rose to the top by a largely natural process.

Barber B. Conable Jr. was born in 1922 in Warsaw, New York, birthplace of the abolitionist Liberty Party. Among his ancestors was Thomas Crafts, one of the True Born Sons of Liberty who in 1765 hung an effigy of stamp-tax distributor Andrew Oliver from Boston's Liberty Tree. The Conables made the trek westward in 1822, as construction of the Erie Canal was opening up the area to settlement.

They became the leading family of Wyoming County, which was sliced off from Genesee County in 1841. Barber B. Conable Sr. was a county judge from 1924 to 1951; his son John succeeded him and served until 1983, which is why lawyers, including Barber's daughter Jane, now go through their motions in the "Conable Courtroom."

The Conable farm bred lawyers. The Conable clan were substantial citizens, but with certain charming eccentricities. The senior Barber Conable recited verse—in particular "The Lady in the Lake"—while milking. "Our cows used to give better to iambic pentameter," says Barber Conable Jr. "They were the most productive cows in Wyoming County."

Young Barber had a prominent surname and a strange forename. "I didn't like my name at all," he says, reciting the childish taunts of seven decades ago: "Barber, Barber, shave a pig, how many hairs to make a wig?" That sort of teasing is helpful in keeping a bright boy just far enough from the pack to develop a critical intelligence. (Though in later years some constituents were sure that they were represented in Congress by a nice lady named Barbara Conable.)

Conable attended Cornell, where, as a good young pacifist, he organized the America First Committee. (One leftist America First ally, a cheeky student of literary bent named Kurt Vonnegut, later "lobbied me about trying to get more deductions for authors.") Then war came, and Conable went. Between service in the Second World War and the Korean War, he earned a law degree. When Uncle Sam let him return home, he hung out his shingle with his retired father as they established the firm of Conable & Conable in the nearest city, Batavia. (Brother John was by now a judge in Wyoming County, and Barber "wasn't about to put myself in the position where all my life I'd have to practice in my brother's court.")

Charlotte Williams, whom Conable married in 1952, was a Buffalo girl, liberated from what Vachel Lindsay called that city of "prosy men with leaden eyes." She and Barber settled into the house at 133 Bank Street, just a couple of lots down from the site of Batavia's most notorious murder.

(In 1883, box-factory owner E. N. Rowell caught his wife in bed with her lover at 123 Bank and shot the man dead. Rowell was acquitted by a jury of sympathetic Batavians in the O.J. Simpson case of the Gilded Age. "I've shot a man," the dazed cuckold told neighbors who heard the shots. "He seduced my wife. I caught him in the very act. I've warned her often. So often." The deceased lay in a pool of blood, fly open, "his penis projecting therefrom." The Batavia jury returned a verdict of not guilty "upon the ground of self-defense" after two hearty minutes of deliberation. The *New York Times* editorialized, "Rowell now goes free on a verdict which is so singularly ridiculous that the whole affair is calculated to place American justice in anything but a pleasing light.")

Young Barber jumped into civic affairs as if he was auditioning for a role in a Sinclair Lewis novel. He was active in Boy Scouts, United Fund, Chamber of Commerce, and the Rotary Club, for which he directed "The Fluorine Follies," a homegrown satire (at a safe distance from Sondheim) on the fluoridation of the water supply.

Rotary would serve as the young man's engine. In Richard Fenno's classic study *Home Style*, Conable credited the Saturday morning donut gang with "propel[ling] me into the Rotary Club over the dead bodies of several local attorneys who had been trying to get in for years, and over the dead bodies of the two attorneys who already were members. It was a key move for me, because it put me in contact with the business community in town—all 120 of them."

In 1962, Conable challenged a corrupt dotard named Austin W. Erwin, chairman of the New York State Senate Finance Committee. The sight of a phalanx of energetic young Batavia Rotarians plumping for their prepossessing paladin—the farmboy lawyer who played viola, loved Schubert, recited poetry from memory, and was to all appearances a loyal and conservative Republican—scared Erwin into retirement. Conable won his maiden race in what the *Daily News* termed "a vote-getting display that left veteran political observers gasping." Signally, he won 329 of the 346 votes in Alexander, fifteen miles north of Warsaw, where he and Charlotte had settled. Thus he came into politics with the most meaningful endorsement—that of his neighbors.

Two years later, after making a rapid mark in the state senate with his heroic defense of rural schools against the Cold War mania of consolidation, Conable was elected to the U.S. House despite the Goldwater debacle. During the next twenty years he would be seriously challenged for reelection only once—in 1974, by the peppery vice mayor of Rochester, forty-one-year-old Midge Costanza, everyone's favorite aunt. (Midge lost and went to the White House with Jimmy Carter, where she wound up in the hot-water wing.)

Well do I recall the fall of 1974, when my brother, Mark Shephard, and I spent hours sticking flyers under car windshields for . . . Midge Costanza. She was a brassy, foul-mouthed (or so I am told) populist, very sweet to us kids when we met her at the St. Nick's Club, sort of an Elks lodge for Batavia's Sicilians. I have never mentioned this to Mr. Conable but . . . well, there you are. I was a teenage liberal.

In many ways Conable was a classic Upstate New York Republican: parsimonious with the taxpayers' dollar, pro–civil rights, and something of a feminist. Charlotte is not just something of a feminist; she was a leading campaigner for a statewide Equal Rights Amendment (which was trounced in 1975) and the author of a book on women at Cornell. Conable's mother was a suffragette; his grandmother was a close friend of Susan B. Anthony. "So I came by it honestly," he says. "I wasn't just being a Milquetoast for my wife's enthusiasm."

Western New York was Margaret Sanger country, and the Conables, like most upper-middle-class Republicans in Genesee County, are staunchly pro-choice and active supporters of Planned Parenthood. The pro-lifers tend to be the working-class Catholic Democrats who are invisible in the national party.

I love the hodgepodge nature of Batavians' politics, which discombobulate those whose misfortune it is to have been formally educated and thus fed into Team A or Team B. The conventional dullards of A and B monopolize American politics: no other teams are ever allowed on the field, and so twenty-four perfectly good letters go to waste. At elite levels, the flavorful and bizarre variety of Batavia politics—of freethinking America—go utterly unrepresented.

For instance, there is no place for Woody, the dreadlocked Christian dairy veterinarian bumping along in his pickup truck listening to Rush Limbaugh—and eloquently denouncing bovine growth hormone and other chemical or genetic manipulations of his patients as ungodly alterations of "their cow-ness." Nor is there space for my placeist friends whose cluster of sentiments—pro–family farm, anti–chain store, anti–gun control, anti–U.S. intervention in other peoples' wars—makes perfect sense to me but perplexes or frightens the NY-DC-LA guardians of acceptable opinion.

I have on my desk campaign buttons promoting two of my favorite modern candidates: an iridescent "Come Home America" pin for George McGovern in 1972, and a stark "Support Neighborhood Schools" badge advertising George Wallace's run in that same year. To me, these are perfect complements: each evinces a love of the local, the particular. The isolationist abhors war because he loves his country; the localist detests social engineering because she loves her neighborhood. (Why is it, by the way, that we isolationists are called xenophobes—when we are the ones who *oppose* killing foreigners? And have you noticed that "Not in My Backyard" is deemed mingy and selfish by the editorialists of the corporate media—the kind of placeless people who never stay in one spot long enough to learn to love their backyard?)

Barber Conable was fairly conventional in his politics, though he had a libertarian streak that kept him admirably distant from the aptly denominated Dead Center. And there was something odd about him, beyond his name. He accepted no campaign contribution of greater than $50, even when Midge Costanza was pounding him for his "blind faith in the innocence of Richard Nixon." (Conable praised Nixon's politics as decentralist, but he never forgave his lies, even refusing to join the fulsome eulogies upon the Trickster's death.)

Almost alone among members of Congress, Conable wrote his own newsletter, which was meditative, never polemical or self-advertising. He quoted Kierkegaard ("success ultimately depends on finding a truth that's true for you") under the frank of the U.S. Congress, and his musings inspired his admirer Senator Pat Moynihan to attempt his own newsletter, which appeared with Halley's Comet–like frequency. (Needless to say, Moynihan's loathsome colleagues and successors—Senators D'Amato, Schumer, and Clinton—have not followed his lead.)

Conable returned home at least forty times a year, where he could be seen scouring gun shows for Indian artifacts and walking his treed 250-acre estate. "It's very difficult with Congress meeting all year long to maintain a personal relationship with your constituency," he says. "You become a shadow on the tube." Especially those who were never all that corporeal to begin with. His district also included the suburbs of Monroe County and part of the city of Rochester, but he confessed to Richard Fenno that he felt uncomfortable among the deracinated middle managers of Kodak-Xerox land: "In the urban area, I'm a captive of the party. I go to rallies and stand up and make platitudinous pro-party solidarity statements. I'm not allowed to be independent, to be myself. People in the rural areas wouldn't be satisfied with this. They expect whole relationships with people, not fragmentary relationships the way city people do. I like whole relationships, and that's why I do so much better in the rural area than in the urban area."

Conable was forgiven his heterodoxies—his feminism, for example—because people *knew* him. In a "whole relationship," a man is more than the sum of his political stances. This is why in Genesee County an atheist homosexual and a fundamentalist Christian can be friends—because they are both so much more than a name tag—while in suburban Virginia or Orlando or San Diego they hate each other's guts.

Conable's successors have been uniformly dreadful time-servers who are about as autochthonous as Blockbuster Video. They are Fred Eckert, a Reaganite who later became ambassador to Fiji; Louise

Slaughter, a party-line Democratic hack; Bill Paxon, a well-scrubbed Erie County boy whose talent was shaking down corporate interests for GOP donations until his sudden resignation in the wake of rumors that his sexual tastes . . . oh, damn those libel laws!; and our current tribune, Paxon's round and bland protégé, Tom Reynolds, who is also talented at turning on the PAC spigot, and is a carpetbagger to boot, having lived outside the district until after he was elected to the seat. But then what does it matter? Slaughter, Paxon, and Reynolds could be from anywhere, which is to say they are from nowhere. They are congresspersons for a global age, as accentless as the computer-generated voice that tells you to watch your step as you board the people-mover within the Atlanta airport.

Conable, contrariwise, was, in an almost organic sense, the representative of the place that was his home.

"It must be terrible to be without roots, without a place to call home," Conable mused to Richard Fenno in the early 1970s, as they drove the back roads en route to a county fair while Fenno was researching his gem *Home Style*. I am in many ways at antipodes from Conable—being an anarchist isolationist part-dago Catholic—yet I revere him. Barber Conable is the only politician I have ever met who could keep me from snorting at the euphemism "public service."

But let us leave the hagiographies to David McCullough, Doris Kearns Goodwin, and the other well-paid courtiers of the PBS history department. Barber Conable was fallible. When the city fathers asked him to secure urban renewal funding, he complied, having no idea that "they were going to put up that mausoleum" of a mall. And he helped pave our road to hell when, as chairman of the Batavia Republican Committee, he foisted upon us the city manager system, which has delivered the daily mismanagement of our city to a series of credentialed outsiders who regard Batavia as just another line on their resumes.

In the late '50s, the young Cornell lawyer "got to looking at Herman Gabriel, who was then the mayor." Herman, a projectionist at the theater, "didn't wear socks when he came to get an award from the Rotary Club," recalls Conable. "Herman was a nice guy who, if somebody called up and complained their garbage hadn't been collected, he'd go and collect it himself. And Batavia was just about wallowing."

Oh, what I wouldn't give to wallow in the Batavia that once was. Conable enlisted the city Democratic chairman, Joe Ryan, and they handpicked a city commission that birthed a new charter, ridding Batavia forever of the possibility that a working-class lunkhead like Herman Gabriel might run things. Recall Pat Moynihan's lament that the small Upstate cities had, to their eternal regret, listened to the progressive young men and not the reactionary codgers.

Moynihan understood better than Barber Conable that sockless Herman Gabriel was just what we needed to avoid the progressive hell of urban renewal. Moynihan also had a charmingly definite notion of what Barber Conable ought to be.

Conable tells this story: "Jack Danforth [R-MO] had a little Social Security amendment that was stupid and wasn't going to go anywhere. We had a conference on the bill that included this amendment of his. Nobody on the House side wanted it, and not many on the Senate side, but Moynihan gets up and makes a speech about this wonderful amendment. Jack was looking over at us and hoping someone would say something on the House side.

"I finally got up and said I hadn't really supported this at the outset, but the more I thought about it, the more I thought it was something we could live with. Pat was sitting at the other end of the semicircle of conferees. He took his pencil out of his mouth, threw it down on the table and it bounced way up. He stalked around the back of the circle, came over and sat in the empty seat next to me and said, 'Now, Conable, are you or are you not an unreconstructed conservative Republican Upstate bastard?'

"I said, 'Now, don't give me a tough time on this, Pat; you supported it.' He said, 'Yes, but I am not an unreconstructed conservative Republican Upstate bastard.'

"I said, 'Well, Pat, you know it's not going anywhere, and I wanted to give a little vote of confidence to Jack Danforth, a sweet man. Don't worry: none of my boys are going to vote for it.'

"And he said, 'Well, Conable, I want to tell you: if you aren't an unreconstructed conservative Republican Upstate bastard, what good are you?' "

Moynihan messed up the details—Conable is a reformist descendant of suffragettes and rural pacifists—but he grasped the larger point. Barber Conable embodied his region. He could no more betray his place than he could alight on Neptune.

Of course, we shall not see his likes again—but isn't it pretty to think so? Our little postage stamp of ground produced the best member of the U.S. Congress, and the homing impulse brought him back. That Conable kid—he ain't goin' nowhere.

CHAPTER FIVE

This Bud's for Us

> I started my first novel at nineteen, in direct response to a
> Jewish girl from New York City who hated "apple-knockers."
> That's what she called upstate New Yorkers. She liked me but
> figured I was an exception. Of course, I wasn't. I had the same
> prejudices—Republican, Protestant, the whole thing. So I tried
> to present a rich vision of the apple-knocker world, openly and
> honestly. I felt when I finished it that the girl would have to
> think after reading the novel that apple-knockers were OK if
> you took time to understand them.
>
> —JOHN GARDNER

Before John Gardner, Batavia's place in American literature was an afterthought, a throwaway. De Tocqueville mentions us in a notebook: "Settled aspect of country as far as Batavia. Scattered houses then marshes. Rooms built of tree trunks." Ah, that incisive Frenchman, trenchant as always!

The Irish poet Thomas Moore spent one night in 1804 in the "miserable little backwoods settlement of Batavia," which inspired him to write "Song of the Evil Spirit in the Woods." At the end of Fitzgerald's *Tender Is the Night*, Dick Diver winds up "in a little town named Batavia, N.Y., practicing general medicine," but even this fame is fleeting. Later in the sentence we learn that Diver relocates to Lockport, which would one day be the hometown of Joyce

BILL KAUFFMAN

Carol Oates. Perhaps Dr. Diver was anticipating the mint to be made by exploiting that exopthalmic's much-chronicled hypochondria. (The city of Lockport's brochure "Notable Lockportians" pictures the supermodel and hemorrhoid-medicine spokeswoman Kim Alexis but not Oates.)

In Paul Horgan's novel of the Southwest, *A Distant Trumpet*, Hiram Hyde Prescott "was born in Batavia, New York," and seasoned "in the intimate and lovely landscape of Western New York." Kurt Vonnegut's *Slapstick* refers glancingly to "Clarence Daffodil-11 Johnson, the chief of police of Batavia, New York," in an obvious nod to John Gardner, who had recently made famous a fictive Chief of Police of Batavia. In Frank Lloyd's western film *Wells Fargo* (1937), Joel McCrea makes a mail drop at Batavia. Okay, I'm stretching. But no more so than our neighbors to the south, the good folk of Wyoming County, who claim Fran Striker, creator of the Lone Ranger, as their contribution to letters. (Striker sold the rights to the masked man for $10; John Gardner died deep in hock to the IRS. Edmund Wilson, too, rather famously forgot to pay his taxes from 1946 through 1955. Upstate literary men should never be trusted with a checkbook.)

Batavia had our own poetic Yates, the anagrammatic kin, at least, to the Irish verse-maker. John Yates was a Methodist minister who lived in the somber brown Gothic home at the corner of State Street and Washington Avenue. He was a hymnodist, first and foremost ("Faith Is the Victory" was his best-known composition), but he also wrote James Whitcomb Rileyesque verse. ("Well, Betsey, this beats everything our eyes have ever seen! / We're ridin' in a palace fit for any king or queen.") His poesy urged regular church attendance and discouraged the use of spirits ("And now the end has come at last, as it doth surely come/To all who bind upon themselves the cruel chains of rum"). I have a copy of his sole book, *Ballads and Poems*, inscribed by the poet weeks before his death in 1900. In the lugubrious springtime I pick up our Yates, his spine detached, pages loose, and read the chorus of his song "Beautiful May":

Beautiful May, life glideth away
We'll meet o'er the river,
My beautiful May

Yates is buried in the Old Batavia Cemetery, under a headstone purchased in 1935 by the ladies of the historical society. Every June, Catherine Roth—to whom one daren't say no—shanghais a dozen or so noble spirits to stand by the graves and impersonate the cemetery's dead celebrities for Batavia's fourth-graders.

Pete Arras, the retired principal who pitched a victory in the first-ever Batavia Little League game, is General John H. Martindale, who defended land claims of the Seneca Indians against the rapacity of the Ogden Land Company. (Pete, a Seneca, is grateful.) Librarian Rita McCormack shushes the urchin horde as the Richmond's first librarian, Mary Elizabeth Wood. Holland Land Office Museum director Pat Weissend is land agent Joseph Ellicott, the dolorous father of Batavia, who established our city's leitmotif by hanging himself in a lunatic asylum.

And Lucine is John Yates, reading from a script by yours truly that relies heavily on gore, for Yates was an accident-prone lad. A rowboat fell on his foot and gave him a lifelong limp. Then, while watching the American Hotel burn, he fell off steps and hit his head on a rock. Best of all, as a sixteen-year-old thespian in the Batavia school play, the clumsy Yates insisted on using a bowie knife in a scene of derring-do. The overacting boy fell on his blade, punctured his lung, and almost died. The kids pepper Lucine with unanswerable questions about the details of the mishaps, and she lies to them as best she can.

Lies, lies, lies: if italicized, the words refer to the title that John Gardner gave to his student notebooks. But they are also a fitting, if disrespectful, segue to Batavia's only contribution to the national arts and letters, the novelist John Champlin Gardner (1933–1982). His works include ten novels, most notably *Grendel*, *The Sunlight Dialogues*, and *October Light*; several books of advice for aspiring writers;

and *On Moral Fiction*, a notorious polemic against what he regarded as the enfeebled and amoral state of contemporary literature.

Gardner, one of the last major American writers to grow up on a farm (perhaps the last, given the disappearance of rural America), lived in a brick farmhouse on a rise in the Putnam Settlement Road just outside Batavia. The family homestead, as he wrote in his magnum opus *The Sunlight Dialogues*, was "solid, unspeakably dignified with its great blunt planes of chalky orange brick, its Victorian porches, its cupola: the most beautiful architecture in the world, symbolic of virtues no longer to be found." The hillock on which the house sits drops slantwise to the road and was "full of snakes," says a family friend with a shiver.

"Bud," as Gardner was known to family and friends, was an Eagle Scout who played in the band and sang in the chorus at Alexander Central School before graduating from Batavia High in 1951. He had transferred to BHS in order to study with music director Frank Owen, whose son, Jim, coached my MacArthur Park midget baseball team in 1969.

Ask a Gardner coeval about the author and you'll hear one word: *weird*. As a child he loved books and opera; as an adult, he was seen roaming the sepulchral Genesee Country Mall in a black cape, like Merlin in search of a vodka and tonic. Gardner meant a lot to me: he was my Joe Louis, my Al Smith, living proof that a lad from Batavia was not debarred from Parnassus, or a suburb thereof. But, I admit, he was weird.

As a weirdo he did not shun the beaux arts. I think of him lugging that French horn to Batavia High, past the sniggering of the hairy-balled jocks who forever taunt band geeks. I find in a 1950 *Daily News* clip that seventeen-year-old John Gardner Jr. sang with a "quartet composed of young people" to the First Presbyterian Friendly Class. He later lied (he told whoppers that put his close friend and compulsive fabulist James Dickey to shame) that he had been a motorcycle champion, a regular Burned-Over Marlon Brando, but he was nothing of the sort. No, John was a winds weenie, his photo nowhere to be found on the football or baseball or basketball pages of the Alexander and Batavia High yearbooks. (He did go out for track, the sport of those culled from the baseball team. His specialty? The longueur jump.)

For all the cowshit and June bugs that flavor Gardner's autobiographical reminiscences, his family were among Batavia's oldest and most accomplished. Great-great-grandfather Moses Taggert was a justice of the New York Supreme Court. His granddaughter—John's grandmother, Alice Day Gardner—was the first woman to practice law in Batavia. Alice cofounded the Children's Home, whose ministry to orphans was subsidized for so many years by Madam Edna (who appears briefly in *The Sunlight Dialogues*).

Alice's husband Fred—the model for the Honorable Arthur Hodge Sr. in *The Sunlight Dialogues*—was a reporter for the *Daily News* before joining the bar; his funeral, prominently covered in his old paper, was attended "in a body" by Batavia Lodge #475, Free and Accepted Masons. An earlier John Champlin Gardner, among the first settlers in Elba in 1809, served in the New York State Assembly.

The Gardner farm was not run on Earl Butz–Archer Daniels Midland hyperefficiency principles. Priscilla, John's mother, was an English teacher, and his father, John Sr., was a loquacious lay preacher: they recited *King Lear* and the Psalms to each other as they milked the cows. Priscilla ran the Presbyterian Church's Shakespeare Club, which has read aloud the plays of Edward de Vere since 1901. (Just kidding.) The Gardners were famous at the Grange for giving their farmhands Saturday afternoons off so that the boys might listen to the Texaco opera on the radio. Just how many did so was never clear. After all, you can lead a hoss to Wagner, but you can't . . .

As an old man, Gardner père used to befuddle the stockboys at Twin Fair, where I listlessly arranged cans of waxed beans on the shelves, spouting at us Burns and Keats and Edgar Guest, for all I remember, as he shopped for cookies.

□ □ □

When you grow up hearing dairy farmers whistling Walter Scott before dawn you understand that high culture might be shared by muck-spattered workaday men lacking graduate degrees. Thus John Gardner's oft-derided habit of putting poetic language or classical allusions in mouths that never have supped in faculty clubs. The drunk junkman Kuzitski quotes Pope in Henry Soames's diner in *Nickel Mountain*; Gardner's farmers and farmwives are always reciting poetry and reading to each other (or to the kine). Ruth Thomas is "sitting on a milkstool" and reading Poe and Wilkie Collins in *October Light*, while old man Orrick (who "owned a small dairy farm a mile outside the little village of Elba") composes poetry on his tractor in the posthumously published *Stillness*.

Verse in the cow barn is as natural to Gardner as was his use of pipe words like "dottle" or his casual mention of the inevitable farming accidents that cost Gardnerian characters their fingers, their hands, their lives.

"Art begins in a wound, an imperfection," wrote Gardner in *On Moral Fiction*, "and is an attempt either to learn to live with the wound or to heal it. It is the pain of the wound which impels the artist to do his work." Gardner suffered his wound on April 4, 1945, and we can be sure that it never healed.

Let the *Daily News* provide the facts:

CHILD DIES IN FALL FROM FARM TRACTOR

6½-Year-Old Son of

Mr. and Mrs. John C. Gardner is

Killed Instantly

OLDER BROTHER DRIVING

Striking his head when he fell from a balky tractor, Gilbert Day Gardner, 6½, son of Mr. and Mrs. John

C. Gardner of Putnam Settlement, was instantly killed at noon today.

The family explained that the boy was riding on a tractor driven by his older brother, John C. Jr., 11½, when it ran out of gas on a hill near the James Hume farm on the Creek road.

The tractor began to jerk and buck and the smaller boy was thrown off, onto the roadway. He was rushed to Genesee Memorial Hospital, but Coroner Raymond L. Warn of Oakfield said that death had been instantaneous and that the boy was dead on arrival at the hospital. He was run over by the cultipacker which the tractor was hauling. The coroner said death was due to a fractured skull. State Police investigated.

The youngsters were en route from the Fred Gardner farm to their home when the accident occurred. The family said that John, Jr., had been driving a tractor for two years and was well experienced in its operation.

H. E. Turner Mortuary handled the arrangements, as it would almost forty years later when the boy who had killed Gilbert killed himself. For those four decades Gardner lived with a guilt more crushing than any cultipacker; how could he not hate himself? "He's blamed himself all these years for what he couldn't possibly have prevented," said his mother, Priscilla, a year before John's death.

John Gardner's best short story, "Redemption," is laceratingly autobiographical. It begins:

> One day in April—a clear, blue day when there were crocuses in bloom—Jack Hawthorne ran over and killed his brother, David. Even at the last moment he could have prevented his brother's death by slamming on the tractor brakes, easily in reach for all the shortness of his legs; but he was unable to think, or, rather, thought unclearly, and so watched it happen,

as he would again and again watch it happen in his mind, with nearly undiminished intensity and clarity, all his life. The younger brother was riding, as both of them knew he should not have been, on the cultipacker, a two-ton implement lumbering behind the tractor, crushing new-ploughed ground. Jack was twelve, his brother, David, seven. The scream came not from David, who never got a sound out, but from their five-year-old sister, who was riding on the fender of the tractor, looking back. When Jack turned to look, the huge iron wheels had reached his brother's pelvis. He kept driving, reacting as he would to a half-crushed farm animal, and imagining, in the same stab of thought, that perhaps his brother would survive. Blood poured from David's mouth.

John's shoulders buckled underneath the blame. "It's not your fault," spoken however truthfully, is cold comfort to a boy who has crushed his little brother's skull.

"Gilbert was the kind of kid who would never hold on," says Marge Cervone, a longtime family friend who once rode on the back of a motorcycle with John, Gilbert, and their dad on a 100-mile trip to Rock City Park. (Marge, who cofounded an NAACP chapter in Batavia in the '60s despite Batavia's almost complete absence of colored people, is locally famous for taking in delinquents: she quit the Gardners' Presbyterian Church over its high-hatting and still bears a grudge because it, like most houses of worship these days, locks its doors during unholy hours.)

So according to Marge, Gilbert was not the sort of six-year-old who ought to be allowed to ride on the hitch joining a tractor to a cultipacker. With the hindsight of half a century, and living in a different world, we might even assign a measure of negligence to the parents. (Why didn't they check the gas?)

John was distraught, beyond solace. He had killed his brother. How can such a sin, even if God and neighbors deem it an accident, ever be expiated? Shortly after the incident he wrote this poem:

My Brother

In two feet water my brother would wade
He'd do it,
All knew it.
No wilder imp was ever made.
'Twas true!
God knew!

My little brother, sweet though wild
Was better far than any child.
With my small brother, Gilbert Day
Oh yes he lived the mischief way.

Every minute sweet and kind
My brother,
Ask mother.
Blessed was the tie that bind
One another
With my brother.

With a will he shot at work and play
Laughing, singing, always gay.
But once he laughed and played too far.
His jolly songs no longer are.

And you wonder why John Gardner drank himself insensible.

◻ ◻ ◻

"I grew up with farmers," said Gardner in a son-of-toil mood. "I learned more from farmers than from professors."

Not that the farmers returned the compliment. In her invaluable history of Batavia, Ruth McEvoy, retired Richmond librarian, wrote of *The Sunlight Dialogues*: "Critics found the book brilliant. Most local readers were not sure what the author was talking about." (The Richmond Library's copy of *The Sunlight Dialogues* is inscribed, "To Ruth, My favorite librarian, John Gardner, April 28, 1973.")

Gardner set two novels in Batavia. In *The Resurrection* (1966), his little-read first novel, a philosophy professor returns home to die. In *The Sunlight Dialogues* (1972), a native son given to Gardnerian disquisitions on order, law, and morality comes home, well, to die. Before his sun goes down, however, he engages Chief of Police Fred Clumly in a series of metaphysical colloquies in our queer old jail, a "brownstone and concrete imitation castle set back among dying elms and maple trees."

This is hardly naked autobiography, but the Hodges are nothing if not Gardnerian in their muck and strangeness. Barber Conable, son of another poetry-reciting dairy farmer, remembers, "My wife and I, after we had been in Batavia about three or four years, looked at each other and said, 'Somebody ought to write about these people.' And we were just astonished when *The Sunlight Dialogues* came out. Of course it really is a novel: he didn't make the most of the opportunities of fact there."

As if returning the unheard compliment, Gardner conceived of the Hodge paterfamilias in *The Sunlight Dialogues* as a grand man who sounds positively Conablian. In an undated letter written when the novel in progress was called *The Devil under the Stairs*, Gardner wrote: "There's this family of Hodges, in Western New York, which radiates from one grand old man, a Congressman of the old-fashioned sort (my grandfather, really): good politician, good reader of poetry, good farmer, lawyer, father, etc."

Gardner can be read, in patches at least, as a regionalist, not only of western New York but of Vermont (*October Light* is awash in autumnal Green Mountain color, its dialectic, not to mention dialect, poised between Ethan Allen and Norman Rockwell). He also wrote bewitchingly of the Endless Mountains of Pennsylvania in *Mickelsson's Ghosts*.

Gardner insisted that *The Sunlight Dialogues* "provides a fine comic history of Western New York and provides the means for a foreigner's understanding the peculiar attitudes of Western New York—attitudes significant, in my opinion, to the 'American experience' in general." If it took 673 pages to teach that Jewish girl about apple-knockers, so be it.

Publication of *The Sunlight Dialogues* inspired numerous hilariously inaccurate stories which claimed that Batavians were reading the bestselling novel frontwards and backwards, matching up fictional characters with their flesh and blood counterparts. In fact, as Miss McEvoy said, no one here could make heads nor tails of it. Rare indeed was the dogged reader who made it past "The Dialogue on Wood and Stone." Anyway, the town had slipped away from him. Gardner remarked to one reporter, "The city where I grew up has vanished from the face of the earth. My children will never see Batavia, N.Y., as I knew Batavia, N.Y. . . . . Only a few buildings are there to remind us of what it was."

The book is dappled with Batavia names, not what you'd expect given Gardner's dismissal of "realistic fiction [in which] you keep mentioning local roads to prove you're in Detroit." But there they are: landmarks ranging from the Blind School (irresistible as metaphor; it offers the finest vista in the city) to Doehler-Jarvis (where my grandfather worked between policing Batavia and selling papers at Marshall's News Store). He drops the names of the Veterans Hospital, Stroh's Flower Shop, Sylvania, the Richmond Library, and all the old streets—Bank, Ross, Jackson, Harvester, Oak, Ellicott, Washington—which are ominously eclipsed by the new: the Thruway across which Tag Hodge painted his graffito.

The real excitement came with the announcement that *The Sunlight Man*, a genuine Hollywood *movie*, was to be shot in Batavia starring Dustin Hoffman and his actorly tics. (Failing to make *The Sunlight Man*, Hoffman jumped the meteorological fence and won an Oscar for *Rain Man*.) The blacklisted Communist Jules Dassin,

Melina Mercouri's husband and a man who "made some of the most entertainingly bad films of the sixties and seventies," in David Thomson's estimation, wrote a Batavia-centric script. But Dassin was staggering from his disastrous black liberation film *Up Tight*, and so *The Sunlight Man* quietly set.

What I like best in Gardner's Batavia books are the offhand Presbo swipes at Catholics. Fred Clumly's cemetery-side observation is a gem: "Used to be Catholics were beaten from the start in a place like Batavia, but Clive Paxton broke that. Now half the richest men in town are Catholics. Bought up all the fine old houses from the families that used to have the money—and pretty well wrecked them. Tear big holes in them for picture windows, cut the trees off the lawns, paint 'em red, that kind of thing. Not that I'm saying all Catholics are like that. Just the way these ones happened to be."

Thus speaketh, perhaps, the first lady deacon of the First Presbyterian Church—*but not the goddam Chief of Police!*

Gardner saw Batavia through his eyes, which are not my eyes. He once said, condescendingly, "In a nice Anglo-Saxon, Welsh community like Batavia, New York, where I was born, everything's fine until the Italians come. The Italians start singing and drinking wine. The Anglo-Saxons and the Welsh of Batavia don't drink wine and they don't sing. Maybe a little beer. There's a problem, right? They're afraid."

First of all: *Welsh?!?* Where is he talking about? Is the midpoint of the Batavia Club and Mancuso's bowling alley the regional office of Plaid Cymru? Welsh? Hey, John . . . read the phone book! We're no more Welsh than we are Albanian.

There is a certain disingenuousness to Gardner's remarks, which read as a defense of Italian demonstrativeness against straitlaced Protestantism. For however loosely laced he may have been, Gardner was a Batavia Presbyterian, and no traitor to his class. No doubt he cringed at the cruder expressions of anti-Catholicism, and wouldn't say "wop" with a mouthful of garlic, but Gardner could hoot at the Eyeties with the best of them.

His Presboisms just keep on coming. From the plainly autobiographical *Stillness*: "Like most people of their general class in the western part of New York State, they liked Indians, disliked Italians, voted Republican, put themselves down on official forms not as 'Protestant' but as 'Presbyterian,' openly loathed labor unions and secretly loathed Catholics."

I delight in such passages, and hand them off every year to Terry McCormack, son of Eire and the Church, usher at St. Joe's, part of Monsignor McCarthy's Hibernian inner circle. Terry delivers them—with grudging snorts—at our wishfully thinking–named "Batavia Reads John Gardner" night.

Just as Sinclair Lewis had his "Sauk Centricities," which gave the ballast of verisimilitude to his Babbitts and Gunches, so is Gardner unmistakably a product of literate Presbyterian Batavia. His Bataviatics dot even the non-Batavia books. An IRS man speaks in a "desperately low-class Italian accent" to the hopelessly in arrears Mickelsson. Professor Agaard says of his son the monster in *Freddy's Book*: "When he was small we had a woman who took care of him, a Mrs. Knudsen. One of those hellfire fundamentalists. I'm afraid she put the fear of the Lord into him. The hellfire part's behind him now—we're Presbyterians." In *Nickel Mountain*, in the Utica train depot, "An angry voice shouted, 'Which car for Batavia?' " The voice is—must be—angry: the detail is telling.

In scaling *Mickelsson's Ghosts* (1982), the thick novel of Susquehanna, Pennsylvania, that Gardner published just before his death on a Susquehanna curve, I came across a reference to "Punk Atcheson, the grinning, freckle-faced, red-headed boy who'd first made friends" with Mickelsson. This gave me a pleasant jolt. For my dad was—is—friends with Punk Acheson (no *t*) of Batavia, who worked at the Veterans Administration Hospital on Richmond Avenue. I went to high school with Punk's son David, with whom we sat at my twentieth high school reunion. David had been in the service, wore a menacing goatee, and struck my wife as having the most interesting visage at the party. "I gotta Xerox this page and have Dad give it to the real Punk," I thought as I read, but I didn't, because in the end these jokes are always on me. Gardner, that crazy writer? Who cares?

The single best Batavia passage in Gardner comes early in *The Resurrection*, a "Christian novel," by Gardner's description, in which James Chandler, a professor of philosophy, returns to his hometown to die. "Batavia had been, in his day, a farmers' city," writes Gardner, "feedstores, farm-machinery places, a plow factory, the Massey-Harris plant," and for spice, Italians on the south side, across the New York Central Railroad tracks.

Chandler walks the Kauffman neighborhood. He strolls "past the house where William H. Coon [the judge and historian of Masonry] had lived once—in his high school days Chandler had accompanied the old man's solos for flute—and past the School for the Blind." But now, he notices, the elms are gone, Main Street has been widened, "mansions turned into restaurants" (for he wrote on the cusp of urban renewal). While Chandler is reluctant to gainsay Progress, he asserts that "it was *not* all right that the narrow old brick street was gone. It was good, but it was not all right. There was not a trace of the comfortable old country town, nothing. Or if that was too strong, there was nothing that didn't stand out like a death's head, a Victorian gable singing Memento Mori above a cheap, glossy storefront."

This was the Progress that Gardner, like all boys raised by the Greatest Generation, was taught to venerate, although the best of them did so uneasily, and with mounting reservations. We read in Gardner's sprawling valediction *Mickelsson's Ghosts*—so unfortunately set in a university, the all-purpose mausoleum of contemporary American prose—of "mighty Binghamton, blasted by the idiocy of Urban Renewal." Mighty Binghamton, mighty Auburn, mighty Batavia: how the mighty have fallen.

Am I being impertinent toward the dead to ask: Where the fuck were you, John? Don't writers have an obligation to the corpses whose conjuring provides their income? You shoulda been on the porch of the Cary Mansion with Lucy Gilhooly. You really shoulda been there, John.

In *The Sunlight Dialogues*, Gardner wrote of two Batavians: "They talked then of politics, in the age-old style of Western New York farmers, arguing shades of a point of view no longer remembered, much less believed, in most of the world." The shades arguing these shades had a kindred spirit in James L. Page, the mad Vermont farmer of *October Light*, who was born on the Fourth of July and blasted his sister's television set "to hell, right back where it come from." The novel sets up my kind of political dichotomy: not the exhausted and inane liberal versus conservative, but rather Progressive vs. Reactionary, as James's sister, Sally, believes in agribusiness, supermarkets, New York City, the Equal Rights Amendment, and nuclear power. That is to say, she believes in the destruction of rural America, and who can blame James for locking her up?

As a born-and-bred hick, no matter how many baguettes he ate at Bread Loaf, Gardner understood that city living dehumanizes: his corpulent good Samaritan Henry Soames in *Nickel Mountain* perceived that "a man could turn into an animal, then. It was something about living in the city, that was all he could figure."

The pretentiously surnamed Stephen Singular, writing in *The New York Times Magazine*, dismissed Gardner as a "rumpled gnome," a freak whose "white hair falls over his shoulders so he looks something like a pregnant woman trying to pass for a Hell's Angel." (A good line, that.) Gardner's real sin, however, was that, "like Tolstoy," who also wrote an unreadable novel titled *The Resurrection*, he "has an anti-city bias (especially an anti-New York City bias)." (The fact that that city's clerisy has an anti-apple-knocker bias is never worthy of mention.)

"A very unpleasant, aggressive young man," Gardner called Singular in an interview in the *New Orleans Review*. Singular was a city boy, no doubt, a smug smarty-pants. "I think big cities like New York or Chicago tend to foster a certain cynicism that's different from a rural upbringing," said Gardner. Whether or not "the highest purpose of art is to make people good by choice," as Gardner wrote in *On Moral Fiction*, the disappearance of rural America (more of our countrymen are in prison than live on farms) makes a renaissance of Gardnerian moralism about as likely as an anti-Masonic restoration.

My favorite summary of Gardner's politics came from a 1977 interview in *The Atlantic*. "I am, on the one hand, a kind of New York State Republican, conservative," Gardner told his interlocutors. "On the other hand, I am a kind of bohemian type. I really don't obey the laws. I mean to, but if I am in a hurry and there is no parking here, I park."

This sort of communal anarchism, respectful of middle-class and town proprieties if not always observant of them, is so perfectly fitted for the Batavia of my imagination that I feel churlish chiding Gardner for his politics. But I will.

He liked Jimmy Carter: a farmer, pious but liberal, distrusted by coastal elites for his rural southern background. ("I told one of my friends in New York, since the New Yorkers all hate Jimmy Carter because he's southern, I told this friend that I really like Carter, that I voted for Carter, and he said, 'Oh yes, of course you would, you're a Republican.'")

In an odd, unpublished essay written during the 1976 campaign, Gardner lauded Carter and Jack Ford, handsome son and mouthpiece of the accidental president, for their lack of cynicism. Gardner's is a gentle piece, calm, soothing in the way that Carter was before his sanctimony sac broke. Its one angry sentence sticks out like Henry Soames's thumb. Referring to the cynical salesmen of decline and decadence, based in "dangerous, nervous cities like New York, Washington, Detroit [Detroit?], and Los Angeles," Gardner writes: "*They* run the newspapers, the TV stations and radio stations, *they* decide what books should get national book awards, what films should get Oscars, what dim-witted nonsense will play in poor idiot Peoria."

How mild this seems today, in the dying years of the American Empire, when only an idiot, a PBS historian, or a senior fellow at a think tank trusts Them. But back in 1976, when bicentennial firecrackers lit the night, this kind of censure had some bite. We might wonder, however, whether Gardner's point was vitiated or confirmed when several months later the National Book Critics Circle selected *October Light* as the best American novel of 1976.

In Gardner's later works, we find the occasional de rigueur put-down of the "religious right," that chimerical bogey frightening to all good liberals everywhere. How easy it is to righteously denounce this band of abominated Americans, most of them rural and small-town Protestants lacking college educations. How simple it is to scorn a people detested by almost every figure of significance in the higher reaches of the corporate, governmental, and academic worlds. No doubt this is Gardner the dutiful book-reading Presbyterian's horrified reaction at being praised for *On Moral Fiction* by the New York chapter of the Moral Majority. His mortification was even more acute when some jackoff ament in the grandiosely named American Nazi Party invited him to don a brown shirt. These fans must have disconcerted him, but as a farm boy—and that rare university novelist with a genuine, inbred feel for rural life—Gardner ought not to have yielded to easy temptation. Like a drunken fuck with a groupie, execrating the poor and marginalized "fundamentalists" is morally lax.

So, too, his snippy collegiate put-down of "the American Rifleman's Association" (what's that? a Chuck Connors fan club?) in "God Damn the Bicentennial," an essay in defense of a noncommercial patriotism that appeared in the *New York Times* retitled "Amber (Get) Waves (Your) of (Plastic) Grain (Uncle Sam)." Gardner grew up in a gun culture—a rural gun culture with a minuscule rate of violent crime—and it saddens me to see him throw in with the yuppies against his own people.

But Gardner's politics could be an interesting mishmash; according to Susan Thornton's memoir *On Broken Glass: Loving and Losing John Gardner* (2000), Gardner harangued his last Bread Loaf conference with a hungover plea for the export of irradiated food, a cause associated with the technology-worshipers of the capitalist right. (The hackneyed quality of Gardner's later views—those of a scrubbed Batavia Presbyterian grown into university lifer—spoil the denouement of *Mickelsson's Ghosts*, as incestuous homicidal wraiths and

Mormon secret agents give way to a crushingly dull solution involving the illegal dumping of chemicals. It's as though Albert Gore hijacked the mystery.)

Maybe it was all the fuddling consequence of the Demon Drink against which John Yates warned. In any event, Gardner's last years were alcoholic blear and dolorous adultery. Susan Thornton (one of those with whom he committed the adultery) writes that in 1980, Joan Gardner, John's first wife and second cousin, hired a pilot. She gave him the job of dropping leaflets on the Bread Loaf campus reading, "Author of *On Moral Fiction* is immoral. A fraud who is late with his alimony, neglects his children." (Rather like Mickelsson, who squandered the money he owes his wife for child support on a cunning teenage whore.)

Gardner claimed that the dissolute professor was based on James Dickey, but few American writers have ever been as deeply in their cups as our John, who could have taught the Elks a thing or two about consumption.

Conspicuous consumption, that is: the old gag "I never knew he was a drunk till once I saw him sober" did not apply to John Gardner. Two months before his end, Gardner was profiled, sympathetically, by Curt Suplee in the *Washington Post*. They met in a bar "in the shadow of the Plaza" in what Ed Abbey called the Vampire City. By chat's end, "the martini count" approached double digits. Gardner, his "boyish face somewhere between Prince Valiant and Mickey Rooney," his "pudgy, grimy hand" greedily grasping the martini glass, slurred out a defense of *Mickelsson's Ghosts*, boasted that he was "the spokesman for Middle America," and, sadly, recanted, in a sloshingly apologetic way, the innerving attacks he had launched on the Writers of the Moment in *On Moral Fiction*. "I thought those guys I don't like were not really liked by readers either," he told Suplee. "I thought it was just a New York establishment con." It was, John, it was! Apologize *for nothing*! And if you find a single reader of Barth or Barthelme in the entire United States of Amnesia, punch him one for me, too.

◻ ◻ ◻

We ought not to lose sight of John Gardner the Good, the faithful son and reckless friend. Virtually every week for the last year of his life he made the 400-mile round trip between Binghamton and Batavia to care for his father, who had suffered a debilitating stroke. Instead of stuffing John Sr. in a nursing home, Gardner rode his trusty steed, a Harley-Davidson Electroglide 1200, to perform heroic acts that put the knights and ladies of his adolescent fantasies to shame. He planted crops, dressed his seventy-one-year-old father, helped him to the toilet, cooked for him and the weakening Priscilla, sturdied him to walk with the aid of a four-pronged cane, and read to him, especially from E. Nesbitt's children's book *The Magic City* and *Treasure Island*. This was Bud the Eagle Scout. Bud the serenader of the First Presbyterian Friendly Class. Bud the heaven-bound.

His fiancée at the time of his death, Susan Thornton, told a small gathering at the University of Rochester that after their marriage, she and John were going to repatriate to Batavia. They planned to move in with the senior Gardners, helping around the farm while John played the role of the Great Man Revenant, perhaps teaching at Genesee Community College. (Marge Cervone, among others, believes that a colon cancer that had almost killed Gardner in the 1970s had recrudesced. Like Professor Chandler in his first novel, Professor Gardner was coming home to die.)

Ms. Thornton shuddered to imagine herself "barefoot and pregnant in Batavia." After all, she had been raised on a tony street in Rochester, "near the George Eastman house," and attended the private Columbia School for budding upper-middle-class neurotics. Such a life in Batavia would have been "hell," she sneered. Hell? *Hell is marriage to you, lady!* Oh, sorry. La Thornton seemed very sincere, and her book, while damning Gardner as an egomaniacal dipsomaniacal megalomaniacal maniac, is nicely written. But dressed-for-dinner alcoholism in country club Rochester is a lot closer to Hades than life on Putnam Settlement Road.

Gardner never made it back to Batavia alive. On September 14, 1982, the same day Princess Grace descended to her new kingdom and four days before Gardner was to make his third "till death do we part" pledge (his marriage to Susan Thornton was to be at St. Paul's Episcopal Church on East Avenue), Gardner's Harley failed to make a curve in Oakland Township in Susquehanna County, Pennsylvania. He was dealt a fell blow by the handlebars. (Pennsylvania roads are notoriously ill-maintained: he'd never have missed an easy curve closer to home, his real home.)

"The afternoon was balmy, bright; the roads were dry," explained his literary executor, Nicholas Delbanco. "He was a cautious and experienced driver, a few miles from home; he swerved—to avoid another vehicle, perhaps?—and fell . . . It is clear he was trying to make it, fighting to survive."

This was not so clear to everyone: Gardner's younger brother, Jim, once speculated, in a speech at the Perry Public Library, that John's death may have been suicide, a logical suspicion given the ubiquity of dreams of self-annihilation in Gardner's fiction. Priscilla Gardner thought that "he must have blacked out or had a heart attack before the accident." Susan Thornton says that he was driving while impaired, if not drunk. In any event, H. E. Turner, the funeral home that embalmed the fictional Sunlight Man after his death on September 13, 1966, did the same for its creator, who died sixteen years and one day later.

John Gardner's funeral was held at the First Presbyterian Church on Main Street, across from the post–Vatican II travesty of my St. Joe's. Four hundred mourners packed the church, most of them locals. The pallbearers were his brother and cousins, not Bill Gass, Stanley Elkin, and the rest of the legion of the walking unread. A cassette tape played John and his son Joel's duet on "Amazing Grace" with French horns, the instrument of deliverance for the boy who kills his brother in "Redemption." Ann Emmans played "The

Old Rugged Cross" on the organ: "So I'll cherish the old rugged cross / Till my trophies at last I lay down / I will cling to the old rugged cross / And exchange it some day for a crown." (Ann recalls this as the most hymn-filled service in the thirty-seven years she has played the organ at Presbyterian funerals. Most of the selections were Welsh, and the assembled Gardners and relatives sang in full throat—the way Italians might.)

In the December following John's death, First Presbyterian thespians put on "The Sam Weber's Toyshop Miracle," a Christian-Jewish celebration of Christmas written by Gardner and his second wife, Liz Rosenberg. J. D. LeSeur starred as Mr. Weber the Jewish toy maker. Proceeds from the play helped buy the church a new Schlicker organ. When Priscilla Gardner died five years later, Ann Emmans would use it to pump out yet another funereal rendition of "The Old Rugged Cross." As she would in 1993, when father John finally followed his two eldest sons to the family plot.

John Gardner was buried next to Gilbert in the Grand View Cemetery on Batavia's outskirts, near Terry Hills golf course and about a nine-iron chip from the Protestant Kauffmans, the ones who never met Rosary-saying Irish Catholic girls. His epitaph is from his elegy for an artist friend, the poem "Nicholas Vergette 1923–1974." It reads, "ALL HE SPOKE OR CAST WAS MYSTERIOUS AND HOLY." (The verse goes on to castigate "the old stiff-minded gods" and the "unduly religious" and praise a deistic "spirit of God as sunlit pastures," all goldenrod and daisies, not a cultipacker in sight.)

The Gardner Papers wound up at the University of Rochester thanks to the assiduous courting of Gardner by Peter Dzwonkoski, the former director of the Rare Books and Special Collections division and a useful name to keep handy when stumped by the question, "Where are the Polish-American intellectuals?" Unlike the Batavia flyboy and World War II hero Eddie Cichowksi, a.k.a. Eddie York, Peter made peace with his consonants.

Box 22 of the University's Gardner Papers has *Vanity Fair* feature written all over it. It seems that in the last months of his life, Professor

Gardner of SUNY Binghamton was harassed by an unbalanced student named William Gere, cousin of the gerbil-fancying Central New York native Richard Gere. I suppose if your cousin was fucking Cindy Crawford you'd stalk a famous novelist, too.

Gere's scrawled missives accuse Gardner of "treason," not for his playfully epigraphic use of the Founding Fathers in *October Light* but for *Grendel*, which Gere judges "contemptible and the work of a traitor." On March 21, 1982, he issues a challenge: "Mr. Gardner, If you're not a chickenshit, you'll face me in a public debate regarding the 'morality' of your 'fiction.' Bill Gere." The derisive quote marks—the puerile punctuative equivalent of "nyah-nyah-nyah-nyah-nyah"—doubtless deterred Gardner from picking up the gauntlet.

For the macabre, there is Box 57—"Contents at Accident." It contains the appurtenances of modern man—keys, an address book, a Pulsar watch smeared with grease, with wrist hairs sticking from the greased band—and Gardnerian touches: a broken pipe, a pocketknife (apple-knocker till the end!). A tan wallet is stuffed with change, American Express plastic, a SUNY ID card picturing Gardner in the typical eyes-upward-to-Heaven pose of the institutional photo, and, chillingly, a yellow scrap of paper with scribbled directions: "Rt 92 toward state line James Woods—Photographer Rt. side just past house curve?"

That last word and question mark—"curve?"—dangle. John Gardner died when he failed to negotiate a curve on Route 92.

How to memorialize a novelist who called your town a symbol of "both spiritual death and the death of civilization"? (Do you blame the Chamber of Commerce for keeping its distance?)

Batavia had sedulously ignored its native son until 1996. Then Charley Boyd, an English professor at GCC and native Ohioan who drove a blue Festiva with a bumper sticker reading "Jesus Was a Liberal," started recruiting volunteers for a Gardner tribute.

The indefatigable Charley and perhaps a half-dozen of us more fatigable sorts have since wreaked Gardner upon his indifferent hometown. We've organized annual conferences, as well as a vivifying series of Gardner events. Batavia actress Bette Smith, a friend and former tenant of Priscilla's, has performed *Days of Vengeance* at the First Presbyterian Church. In this one-woman play, which Gardner wrote for his mother, a farmwife fends off a rattlesnake as well as her children's serpentine attempts to remove her to a rest home.

The Richmond Library's Paula Meyer brought Joan Gardner back to Batavia to speak, with tang but not bitterness, about her ex-husband. At Peter Dzwonkoski's urging, the University of Rochester published *Lies! Lies! Lies!*, the journal Gardner kept as a sophomore at DePauw University. (He would transfer to Washington University in St. Louis the next year.) The GCC theater students mounted a vigorous performance of James Still's adaptation of *In the Suicide Mountains*. In June 1999, some aerosol-gunning holy vandal even spray-painted "Love" at the intersection of Oak and Richmond, in front of Frank Homelius's old house.

But the road was being repaved, and "Love," as is so often the case, was here and then it was gone.

"Batavia Reads John Gardner" we lyingly call our annual October evening of Gardner lections. In a spirit that I hope is more Jack Kerouac than *Friends*, we schedule the Gardner readings in a coffeehouse. Twice the venues have closed in the week before the event—this is Maxwell House dripping through Mr. Coffee territory, not Seattle, thank God—but we managed. We finally seem to have found a permanent home at the Coffee Spot—in Le Roy.

The annual roster of readers is perhaps ten, with another ten auditors thrown in. No Gardners read, although Maureen Maas-Feary's dad worked on the Gardner acreage as one of those fabled Texaco opera–listening farmhands. And at our first evening, Susan

Thornton sang a movingly tremulous selection from *Marvin's on "The Distant Shore,"* a musical comedy cowritten by Gardner.

Sandy Hiortdahl always wears a black leather motorcycle jacket on which Gardner's shaggy visage was painted by an ex-boyfriend. She is the only reader in the sartorial spirit of Gardner, who once said: "In those days I would wear a crushed velvet robe—I'm shameless, right!—with a huge silver chain. I felt that every time I did a reading, I was cheating the people because they came hoping for something very exciting. I wanted them to think that their $5 or $7 or whatever was worthwhile. So I wore this robe, so that when they went home, at least they could say, 'I went to the most boring reading in history, but, boy, did that guy dress funny!' "

We also sponsor a John Gardner Society creative writing contest for high school students. Our first year we had but one entry, a literate one, thank God, but after that rough start the poems and stories have trickled in, perhaps twenty a year, of various merit.

Little did I suspect that the teenagers of Batavia were so misunderstood. "My life sucks so much I [*sic*] rather die," wrote one saturnine diarist. I wish we might have shone a ray of hope wrapped 'round a $100 bill her way, but alas, her effort was much too [*sic*].

My vote was determined that year when Lucine, looking over the entries, said, "Oh, that's Annie. She's such a good girl. Her mother has multiple sclerosis and Annie pushes her wheelchair everywhere." As vote counter and caster of the final vote, it became my mission to get Annie (whose poem I liked anyway) into the win, place, or show pool. Which I did, the lessons of my professor and famed game theorist William Riker coming in handy yet again.

For years I had whined ineffectually that Gardner was not read in our schools. The Gardner revival has taken care of that. Now, each winter, as many as 700 fifth- to seventh-graders throughout the county illustrate scenes from Gardner's children's story "Dragon, Dragon"—which we, Your Kindly Liberal Censors, have pruned by one sentence. (The one in which the nasty dragon "changed house numbers around so that people crawled into bed with their neighbors' wives.") A blizzard of orange dragons and yellow princesses brighten the walls of the Children's Room at the Richmond Library as the nation's one and only Gardnerian actress, Bette Smith, performs her athletically comic version of "Dragon, Dragon."

I watch, having shirked most of the available responsibilities, and think, *This* is a Resurrection. Kids reading Gardner; kids seeing Gardner performed; kids wearing the "Dragon, Dragon" T-shirts designed by Don Carmichael. Gardner once was lost in Genesee, but now is found. From small things, baby, big things one day come.

If things are not quite looking up around here . . . oh hell, scatter the gloom, Bill: things are looking up. One of these years we'll even get around to putting Gardner's silhouette on a vintage blue historical marker. We've got a site reserved in front of Chief Clumly's jail, an apt spot chosen after a Batavia official told Charley Boyd that a sign posted at the city limits declaring Batavia "Home of John Gardner" did not fit his "vision of where Batavia is going." (Which is going, going . . . gone.)

"I think a writer who leaves his roots leaves any hope of writing importantly," said Gardner, and while he was seldom if ever tristful about the old home place, all weepy and adust about orange gloamings on the Putnam Road, he is back among us, for good, and despite what the Scripture says, he is not exactly without honor in his hometown.

CHAPTER SIX

Wal-Mart Cometh

It seems that whenever Batavia has made a decision,
time proves it to be the wrong decision.
Time and time and time again.

—STEVE CARR

L ooking through *Batavia*, a string-tied sheaf of photographs
of "Prominent Batavians" from 1902, I am struck by how
few of the old names survive in our town. Immobility is
among our virtues, but as is so often the case, it is a quality confined
mainly to the working and peasant classes. The names of the mus-
tachioed doctors and lawyers and satisfied burghers studding the
"Board of Trade"—Griswold, Washburn, Burkhardt, Pease, Tomlin-
son, Rowell, Bidwell, Bigelow—are as vanished as the Anti-Masons.
Just two names endure—R. E. Chapin, namesake of the manufactory
that employs my friend Mike Sheehan, and P. W. Minor, founder of
the shoe factory that still bears his name. (The Minors survive thanks
to their nimble shift into the orthopedic market of "shoes for sick
feet.")

Claude Leland Carr is not pictured in *Batavia*. He would not
found C. L. Carr Co. department store until 1915, ten years after he
left Knoxville, Pennsylvania, for our El Dorado on the Tonawanda.
The newly arrived Carr managed the Oliver & Milne Co. dry goods
store at 107 Main Street, within spitting distance of the Woman's

Christian Temperance Union drinking fountain, whose Hebe-topped geyser sated thirsts wholesomely until the city widened Main Street in 1940 to satisfy the unquenchable thirst of Progress, our true and only goddess. Whereupon the fountain was removed; Hebe was sacrificed to a World War II scrap metal drive.

In 1915, the go-getter Carr tried to buy out Oliver & Milne, whose "success was due entirely to Mr. Carr's hard work and attention," as C. L.'s son Robert wrote with filial pride in his brief *History of Carr's*. But the partners would not sell. So C. L. bought out a nearby bankrupt store at 101 Main, named it for himself, and opened for business. (Oliver & Milne "closed in 4 or 5 years," noted Robert Carr without comment.) The second floor of Claude Leland's new store was leased by the Day & Gardner law firm, whose fitfully lawful descendant John Gardner would novelize Batavia.

C. L. Carr gradually bought up the surrounding businesses on Main and the perpendicular Jackson Street, so that by the 1930s his was the largest store in town. The junior half of our great father-son architectural team, Henry and Frank Homelius, remodeled the three floors of the interior. The facade was redone in a cream-colored Norris stone which, together with the arcade windows and walnut woodworking, informed the customer, "This is a classy place; don't go trying to bargain down the price of millinery."

Batavia's Finest Store (the gift-wrap boxes even said so!) vended men's, women's, children's, and infants' wear, hosiery, silverware, glassware, and furniture, draperies, and blankets. (C. L. launched a "blanket club" in 1923, selling four hundred woolen blankets for 50 cents down and 50 cents a week thereafter; this "original blanket club" brought him "immediate fame throughout the entire retailing world," gushed *Merchants' Trade Journal* in 1954.)

In later years, refrigerators and the idiot boxes that would consume American life were also sold at what was the biggest department store between Rochester and Buffalo. Carr's had class, and Carr's had style, though in the 1960s it had suffered an unfortunate remodeling job by one of C. L.'s sons, an architect who had fled his native heath for New York City and eye-defying functionality. The recessed entryway was squared: mustn't waste any space. Ka-ching, ka-ching, sang the cash register king.

The Carr men were practical, business-minded, and given to membership in Batavia Lodge #475, F.A.M.; the wives tended to be *spirituelle*. Robert's wife, Lucille, conducted poise classes for the lasses of Carr's and founded the Batavia Players in 1931–1932. (Our thespian troupe thrived until the 1960s, when "enthusiasm began to falter," writes Batavia historian Ruth McEvoy, and "young men moved away." But the ineffable Wanda Frank revived the Players in the 1970s, packing the house at John Kennedy School with *Our Town*, *Little Women*, and a series of Frank-penned works.)

C. L. Carr dropped dead of a heart attack in 1947. His son Robert, who was not reluctant to mention his graduation from Massachusetts Institute of Technology, succeeded him, prosperously. He handed off the baton to his son Steve in 1983.

Lucille Carr "was not really a doting mother," says Steve, delicately. "When I was two months old I was turned over to a nanny and my parents went to South America for two months." The Carrs, like so many well-off families at the apex of the American Century, believed in boarding schools, as though stripping a child of his attachment to place and family would strengthen rather than enfeeble a boy. So Steve was shipped off to Ridley in St. Catharines, Ontario. After his graduation from Syracuse University, where he studied history, Steve repaired helicopters in Vietnam. Contrary to Hollywood, upon coming home he was neither spat upon by strung-out peaceniks nor fellated by Jane Fonda: instead, he worked for several months at Biers Department Store in Niagara Falls, learning the ropes, before returning to Carr's in 1973. (Biers, in the melancholy coincidence that is modern Upstate's hallmark, was displaced by the Cataract City's disastrous urban renewal program; it died soon thereafter, a failed mall its ultimate bier.)

Steve and his wife, Beth—a Connecticut girl with a finishing school accent—had the misfortune of taking over Carr's just as small-town America's independent department stores were heading like so many current-borne barrels for the falls. Nevertheless, even into the early 1990s, Carr's maintained its position as Batavia's Finest Store. Beth understood that Carr's was a touchstone. "A girl may buy her first-day-of-school dress here, and then her wedding dress when she gets married, and later a bonnet for her baby. This is an emotional continuum of people from generation to generation," she said in happier times, upon the store's seventy-fifth anniversary in 1990, before the plunge into the rocks.

"We've often thought of having a picnic and inviting everyone who's ever worked here, and we'd probably represent every family in Batavia," said Beth. She wasn't exaggerating, though the collective visages at such a picnic would hardly represent our not always fair-complected city. You see, Carr's hired only the prettier teenage girls. Only the finest faces for Batavia's Finest Store. You could bet your ass that the high school senior ringing up your purchase of notions and lotions didn't have a forehead sculpted by fetal alcohol syndrome.

Lucine worked in the children's section of Carr's in 1991–1992, a service-sector experience she has never let my shiftless, no-good, no-account self forget. But out of this crucible of the soul (for who can wait on the snooty wives of alcoholic chiropractors and not go mad?) came our friendship with the Mumfords.

John Mumford of Detroit played on the University of Michigan football team with a genial center named Gerald Ford. You have heard of one but not the other, and while I bear no animus against the estimable Ford—the best, or shall I say least bad, president of my lifetime—a maliciously invidious comparison is in order.

Jerry made all-American; John rode the bench. Jerry married a divorced lush who made it oh so easy to spend two hundred days a year on the road. John married a pretty pianist and Wolverine coed named Virginia Carr, daughter of C. L. Jerry Ford tried to impeach Justice William O. Douglas for contributing a polemical attack on the U.S. Forest Service to a nudie magazine. John Mumford gave Uncle Scam his due in the U.S. Navy and moved to Batavia to work for his father-in-law's business. As vice president and chairman of the board, John Mumford managed Carr's for forty years with scrupulous honesty and a wry humor that he retained well into his eighties, despite macular degeneration and the desolation of widowerhood.

John is the best advertisement for the erstwhile American middle class, which could be substantive and decent and often delightfully witty and well-read. Jerry, however, was the kind of phlegmatic family-ignoring slug who invariably floated to the top in Cold War/ Organization Man Amerika. I suppose the compare and contrast collapses in the postscript—the companies both men ran fell apart, Carr's with a sad grace and U.S. Inc. in blood and vulgarity. But then, everything falls apart, doesn't it?

On the distaff half, Virginia Carr Mumford painted landscapes (she studied with Roy Mason's sister, Nina) and composed hymns (Ann Emmans played one—"Prayer Is a Golden River"—at Virginia's funeral at the Presbyterian Church). Lonely Betty Ford stayed stewed as Jerry the stud satisfied the Pentagon and ignored his wife. You tell me who the all-American was.

John Mumford had been an assistant manager at Firestone in Akron, Ohio, before Pearl Harbor, and he could have chosen a post-war life in the rootless managerial class. Maybe his kids could have gone to school with the guys in Devo. But he came home with Virginia, surviving the usual misgivings and My God What Have I Dones? Batavia was "the unfriendliest city," he recalled, until he had established his place among us, his permanence. Once settled, he had no regrets, he said, and I believe him. "He was the nicest man at Carr's," says an old customer. The droll Wolverine was always ready with a smile; he was a kindly complement to the more assertive MIT man, Robert Carr.

A week before John's death last February, he told us with a weak smile that he wanted to live long enough to pick one more dandelion.

He died on the warmest weekend of an unusually mild winter. Improbable February dandelions yellowed the fields.

John's son Peter, or Petermumford in our daughter's portmanteau pronunciation, graduated from BHS in 1965. (No Canadian prep schools for the Mumfords.) Peter was and remains a wistful idealist: after Michigan State he joined the Peace Corps and served in Upper Volta (now Burkina Faso to you, white man). For his life of service Peter was named a BHS Distinguished Graduate in 2000. Peter is blessed with the mechanical ingenuity common to Carrs. He worked in New England learning carpentry and other crafts until 1989, when age and creeping decrepitude had slowed his folks, whereupon as the only unmarried child he came home to Batavia to live with them, care for them, save them from the indignity and drool-soaked bedlam of the nursing home. It was an act of love and sacrifice, and it explains why Peter, a good-natured agnostic to his late Presbyterian mother's eternal consternation, is heaven-bound.

Among Peter's mates in the class of '65 was Terry Anderson, an invisible high school geek from the margins who after a stint in the service worked his way up to become the chief Associated Press correspondent in the Middle East. In March 1985 he was taken hostage by the usual aggrieved Arabs; his fifteen minutes of fame would stretch into almost seven years on the cross. The corporate media always identified Anderson as a native of Batavia, though few people recalled him. He had been raised in nearby Albion and only lived in our town for his pustuled high school years, which he spent castling in the chess club and being ignored by the olive dream Italian girls. (Not to worry, Terry: twenty years after they snickered behind your back they were so rotundly maternal they couldn't give a fifteen-year-old boy a hard-on.)

Anderson left Batavia and never looked back, but the TV newsreaders told us that he was a Batavian, and our town was depicted as a place right out of Andy Hardy, where Boy Scouts (not speed-popping Mickey Rooneys) and busty virginal gals (not depressive sluttish Judy Garlands) were waiting at the soda fountain for

Terry to come marching home again, hurrah! hurrah! Well, he did. Anderson was released at the end of 1991, and the network aliens descended on Batavia, cameras on shoulders and microphones in hand, to capture the weeping, the shouts, the unadulterated joy. At 6 P.M., the church bells throughout town rang in unison for the first time since V-J Day. I walked downtown, through the blowing snows of an early December storm, to hear the peals from the adjacent Presbyterian and Baptist churches on Main Street. There were two or three other auditors, that's all. We listened for a while and went home. Later that night, a restaurant threw a heavily advertised open party, which thousands of jubilant Batavians and assorted freeloaders were expected to attend. To the vexation of the Celebrity Nation, about seventy-five showed up.

Does this mean that we are unneighborly, or snow-shy shut-ins, or that we refuse offers of free pizza and beer? No. The genuine excitement had occurred the weekend before, as thousands had made the trek to Rich Stadium, home of the Buffalo (*sic*: not a single player is indigenous; if only pro sports had territorial drafts) Bills, where the Batavia Blue Devils football team beat Grand Island for the state's Class B high school championship. These people had chosen real life, the ties of blood and kith and kin and authentic community, over the unreal and insubstantial images and artificial emotions that TV had conveyed.

Batavians were pleased that Terry Anderson was coming home— wherever home was to this foreign correspondent. (He did not settle here.) But we did not know him, and he did not know us. He was an image on a TV screen, no more actual than Peter Jennings. I was proud of both our collective indifference to Anderson and the city-wide frenzy over the football team. BHS! BHS!

Anderson, by the way, handled his awkward homecoming with grace. So did his energetic Batavia advocate, the admirable Ann Zickl, daughter of the last state Supreme Court justice these voteless parts will ever produce. This is a woman whose good works and volunteer labors give Batavia heart.

Despite Batavia's failure to give Anderson a Hollywood-approved homecoming, the cheerleaders made quite a fuss over the returned prodigal at Terry's delayed twenty-fifth high school reunion. Not all of us are unbelievers in the national religion of TV. A few minutes on the tube and the most hopeless nerd acquires the magnetism of celebrity, pulling his erstwhile tormenters and neglectors toward him like so many iron filings.

Petermumford kept his distance at that reunion, but then he has a natural dignity.

Petermumford helped at the store when he could. He befriended Ben, the store's temperamental Buffalo-based window designer. (When the mood strikes, Ben is sometimes known as Lauren Fox. Ben/Lauren was a sashay-on in the draggy film *To Woo Fong, Thanks for Everything! Julie Newmar*.) Peter and Ben made 20-foot-high nutcracker soldiers—don't think the entendres weren't doubled over in the art room that day—that stood sentry outside Carr's at Christmastime throughout the 1990s. Ben used to sunbathe in his underwear on the Carr's roof, a spot shielded from all but the prying eyes of degenerate Masons atop their temple. (Ben's trail is throughout the warehouse and crannies of Carr's: yellowed cheesecake shots from men's magazines tacked to walls.)

Petermumford was a director and stock owner of Carr's, though that latter distinction is not unlike being a Confederate banknote hoarder in 1867. Spooked by his first heart attack, C. L. incorporated the business in 1946, limiting the stockholders to members of the Carr, Mumford, and Minor families. It was an authentic family-held company in the best Middle American tradition—but like all traditions in the Land of Silk and Money, it up and died.

❏ ❏ ❏

In 1992, Wal-Mart Cometh—all 116,000 square feet of it. The Arkansas weed sent up shoots across western New York in the turbid Clinton Dawn. Construction in Batavia "received only minor opposition from those living nearby who feared increased traffic and a disruption of the area's rural setting," according to Kevin Saville in the *Daily News*. The silence of Wal-Mart critics spoke volumes. Let the wind blow a stray Wal-Mart plastic bag within fifty miles of Vermont and the yuppies (if not, significantly, the natives) are up in arms: hereabouts, Beth Carr complained, Landmark Society members and Batavia patriots grumbled. But respect for Free Enterprise (even in ersatz and hypertrophied form) is such that denying Wal-Mart a building permit seemed . . . socialistic. And besides, they sell jeans and shoes and charcoal grills cheaper than Carr's and Genesee Hardware and the diminishing downtown remnant. (Never mind that Wal-Mart is an excrescence of a grand Republican experiment in state socialism, the Interstate Highway System.)

My voice was as mute as the others in that silent night, unholy night. I suppose I am of the old New England school of Thoreau and Emerson in that I distrust political solutions and prefer individual revolutions of the soul. I sympathized with those townspeople who wished to keep Wal-Mart out. But instead of passing laws to compel behavior I would much rather that my neighbors *choose* to shop locally. They will only do so when Batavia becomes once more a city with its own flavor and fashions. Whether that day will come I do not know.

The first casualty of the Arkansas behemoth was Newberry's, Carr's Main Street neighbor, a dime store with a '40s-ish lunch counter. (In reveries I see Gloria Grahame spinning on a Newberry's stool, skirt hiked, smacking her lips over a tuna sandwich.) When Newberry's closed around Christmas 1995, Diane Bartz Keicher wrote a poignant letter to the *Daily News*:

> If I could have just one Christmas wish, it would be to see Batavia just one more time the way it was—Batavia in its splendor, Batavia alive again! If I could just show my husband and children what a beautiful city it once was; if I could just walk

down Main Street at this Christmas season and have them experience with me how special it was.

But this will never be: our beautiful downtown is gone and
we will have to be content to shop the Wal-Marts and Kmarts
or the malls in some other city. (We do still have C. L. Carr's,
thank goodness!) But our children will never know the "homey,
warm, small-city" feeling that Batavia once had and could have
still had.

We did still have C. L. Carr's, thank goodness. But goodness
wasn't enough.

So why did it matter anyway? Who cared if one bought shirts from
Wal-Mart rather than Carr's?

I'll tell you what difference it makes, in anecdotes big and small.
(Anecdotal evidence is always superior to statistics: numbers lie,
trust the eye.) And speaking of eyes, for close to three decades
Ralph Huber at Batavia Optical has fixed the glasses whose bows I
am always breaking and pins I am forever losing—and he does it
gratis, with just a handshake and smile and "Thanks, Bill." Wanna
try walking into the Vision Center chain with disassembled specs
and having them put Humpty Dumpty back together again on the
spot, and for nothing? You're as likely to bump shopping carts
with that flathead social climber Martha Stewart in the linens aisle
at Kmart.

On a larger scale, I have mentioned previously the tractor factory
that had been founded by the Allans of Batavia, sold to Yale and
Towne, and merged with the Eaton Corporation of Cleveland before
being purchased by a German firm. The Germans fired those salaried
employees who were within a few years of a full pension. (These
included my father, a draftsman.) The Krauts did so without repercussion, for Batavia was no more real to them than an image on a
computer screen. Just press DELETE and we vanish. Contrast this with
the efforts of Steve Carr to keep open his failing department store.

Or consider the neighborliness of the Carrs when my dad's cousin, the irrepressible Eddie Ballow, discovered that a deceased and destitute relative, the black ewe of our family, had left a cairn of unpaid bills. Eddie, impelled by no compulsion but family honor, went around making good on the dead deadbeat's debts. Except at Carr's, which in the spirit of Christian charity simply wiped the debit off its books. Try that at Wal-Mart.

(Eddie, the former dog warden of Akron, New York, stars in a favorite anecdote of our friend Lou Nanni. It seems that a stray German shepherd was barking and growling its way down the Nannis' street, and Eddie came by to detain the canine fugitive. He cornered it in the Nannis' backyard. The dog, half feral, resisted arrest. Mrs. Nanni thought bait might break the Mexican standoff.

"Mr. Ballow," she shouted from the door, clad in a nightgown, "would you like a hot dog?"

Eddie, concentrating on the snarling cur, gave her a brief glimpse of incredulity. "Not now, thanks. Can I take a rain check?")

□ □ □

Conventional retailing wisdom supplies a standard strategy for battling Wal-Mart: beat a hasty retreat to a niche as yet unoccupied by the invader. Say, upscale clothing. Carr's eschewed this tack, on the grounds that Batavia hadn't enough of a yuppie market on which to subsist. "They started stocking junky stuff," says one longtime shopper, and no one can whip Wal-Mart in a junkyard fight.

Steve fought back as best he could. When Newberry's closed, and its popular lunch counter with it, Steve tried to sell coffee (he did not, thankfully, call it javahh!). He closed Carr's second floor, and then the basement, bailing water and scrambling for a toehold on the shrinking deck of his sinking ship. He opened the store on Sundays near Christmastime, even though he regarded doing business on the Sabbath as "cutthroat" and "uncivilized." Carr's spent the 1990s slowly drowning in the sort of red-ink sea that even Yahweh couldn't part. Steve dug into the family fortune to keep from laying off the store's longtime employees. Anyone else—anyone whose name was not emblazoned on the storefront—would have given up by 1995. Yet he pushed on, customerless, hemorrhaging cash, in the way that only the bearer of an Old Family surname can: to certain defeat, honorable defeat. Middle-class Batavians drove the thirty miles to the suburban malls; working-class Batavians, some resenting the uppityness of Carr's past and taking a certain satisfaction in seeing them laid low, our own not-so-Magnificent Ambersons, packed the parking lots of Wal-Mart and Kmart.

Steve, the only son of Robert and Lucille, was born a Carr and bred for Carr's: "My father very much wanted me to carry on the family name. He was delighted when I came in." But as the store stalled, one heard grumblings that this Carr had no key.

"Steve's got to learn to be practical," said one architect of that downtown renaissance whose arrival could tax the patience of a Jehovah's Witness. "He can't run the business like his grandfather did. Times change."

As the end draws nigh, I ask Steve's critics to let fly. They do:

"Steve's lazy."

"Born with a silver spoon."

"Spoiled."

"He never wanted to be in retail."

Maybe. Maybe not. But the dignity with which he held on past the point of all hope—"If it was purely a business decision, it would have been made a long time ago," Steve said of the closing when it inevitably came—made him noble in my eyes, the Last of the Department Store Mohicans.

Lest our vision become clouded by Morning in America mist, I must point out that Carr's paid the help peanuts. More than one "associate," as department stores patronizingly term their employees, jumped ship for the iniquitous Marts. And much as my own biases push upon me the Goliath crushes David story of a doughty local patriot vanquished by the corporate behemoth, facts do have an inconveniencing way about them. After all, Steve was educated at Ridley in Canada instead of good old BHS. His two sons also avoided the local academy. Steve and Beth sent their boys to Rochester's tony Harley School, which accepts shopkeepers' sons but has no shop class. Moreover, on my last visit before The Awful News, Steve urged me to dump our Internet provider, the Main Street son of my old gym coach, and sign up with Time Warner.

But now back to our regularly scheduled morality play.

Steve ran the show and kept the dismaying books from the third-floor office, with its exquisite design by Batavia Woodworking, its glass cases full of Carr's memorabilia from flusher times, and its pneumatic vacuum tubes that swooshed money, like a vertical ATM, from the first floor to the third floor. (That was back when Carr's had money enough to swoosh.) The last time I saw Steve before The Announcement I had stopped by to pay our monthly bill—in person, Steve stamping it "paid," just like Sam Walton's ghost doesn't do. Steve, whose talented son Ted is a budding actor, was listening to the CD soundtrack of Rochester's version of *Rent*, a musical titled *Convenience*, with its obligatory theme of homosexual love. Steve hummed the cocksucking threnody under the disapproving gaze of a Nina Mason Booth portrait of stern old C. L. Carr.

"Wow. How un-Rotary," I thought, but it really isn't. How could I forget the disastrous staging of *Side by Side by Sondheim*? Might *Convenience* be the next boundary transgressed by the intrepid Rotary Club troupe?

Steve needed whatever musical talisman he could find to ward off the Black Death that had in rapid succession claimed Marshall's News Stand, Sleght's Book Store, Beardsley's clothing shop, and even the empire of the Mancusos, the Sicilian moguls who in recent years have lost Mancuso Motors, Mancuso Plumbing, Mancuso Furniture, and now even the Mancuso Theater. (The last-named was sold by one branch of the family to City Church, a growing evangelistic congregation led by "Pastor Marty.")

Now, one might think that preserving the extruding "Mancuso" marquee would be of interest to those who owe their greens fees and Bills tickets to the Founding Generation. But ancestor worship is the one vice from which the Third Generation is immune. Don't look back! Keep your eyes on the Glorious Future! Change is Good! Change is God! (In the interest of fair play and ethnic amity, I hasten to point out the manifold charitable contributions made by various of the Mancusos, whose surname says "Batavia" as strongly as Adams says "Boston.")

In early 2001, the city's toothless Historic Preservation Board, stacked with our preservationist friends, tried to designate the Mancuso Theater a historic landmark. This would have forbade the removal of the marquee or the effacement of the facade's bas-relief mermaid that is Batavia's topless contribution to art moderne.

The public hearing on the designation took place in old City Hall while City Church and the Mancusos were in negotiation, an unfortunate bit of scheduling that made it look as though the Historic Preservation Board was trying to queer the deal. Which it may have been. Batavia's Collegiate Class has the usual anti-fundamentalist Christian bias. This parti pris was only deepened when a churchman suggested as an alternative to the erasure of the mermaid her transmogrification into "an angel." Wearing a heavenly bra, surely.

Threatened with a lawsuit by the Mancusos, the preservation board retreated; the theater was sold, consecrated, and we prepared to mourn. The last marquee in town would be carted off to the junkyard, and the mermaid's aquatic curves would be forever sandblasted away. But they were not—for the Lord works in mysterious ways—and the good folk of City Church saved the marquee and the mermaid, who was repainted a demure tan.

On a gray May day, Lucine and I peeked into the quondam theater as workmen remodeled it into City Church. Steve Carr joined us. The sanctification of Mancuso's was well under way: the bas-reliefs along the wall had been sanded away, and the two pediment-mounted nude statues of movie palace days were wearing shirts, lest carpenters be beguiled into nipple-induced boners. Yet all in all, the theater-to-church modification seemed a nice example of what the preservationists call adaptive reuse. The ecclesiastical style was more than mere Kmart Revival.

City Church was keeping the theater seats, though a clearing had been carved out: "That's so they can writhe on the floor," said the Episcopalian Steve. Doing his best Ernest Angley, he cuffed me on the head as if I were a crippled cracker. "Spirit be gone!" I said. Within six weeks, Carr's was gone. Out with the Episcopalian, in with the Pentecostal.

❏ ❏ ❏

Petermumford gave Lucine the bad if unsurprising news in early May 2001: Carr's was closing July 17, birthday of Deron Johnson, Don Kessinger, and my brother, Mike. (We kept track of such things as boys. I share November 15 with Bobby Dandridge.) We were to keep the news under our hats, as Steve was ashamed of his failure. He also dreaded the Buffalo and Rochester TV stations carrying maudlin reports about the death of Batavia's Finest Store. Not to worry, Steve: the stations, owned by remote communications conglomerates, prefer not to acknowledge the funerals as the last of the independents die off.

Steve made The Announcement on the Tuesday after Memorial Day. With my usual mistiming, I was in Dixie, interviewing American historian Forrest McDonald (who writes his books in the nude) and staying with Lucine and our daughter, Gretel, in a bed and breakfast in Tennessee Williams's hometown of Columbus, Mississippi. We dozed in a bed in which '50s sci-fi queen Barbara Rush (*It Came from Outer Space*; *When Worlds Collide*) had once slept, sans alien, and of course sans Tennessee.

Steve broke the news to the store's twenty-some employees in a morning meeting on the first floor. He stood by the balky elevator that once creaked and groaned as it ascended from floor to floor with all the celerity of Franklin D. Roosevelt climbing the stairs. The employees were saddened, but hardly shocked. It was a long time coming.

Steve's statement to the press was gracious, without the twist of gall that others might have added: "Speaking for all our valued employees, who have become friends and more like family, we will all miss our faithful customers and friends. They have continued to support the store and helped to 'keep the faith' to keep open what we think may be the last independent department store in the state. . . . On behalf of myself and my family—the Carrs, the Mumfords and Minors—I want to thank all current and former employees, suppliers and customers of C. L. Carr Company for their loyalty, service and patronage."

On the first weekend of June, the "Going Out of Business" signs appeared in the windows of C. L. Carr Co. William Cullen Bryant thought June the best month in which to die (" 'Twere pleasant, that in flowery June / When brooks sent up a cheerful tune / And groves a joyous sound / The sexton's hand, my grave to make / The rich, green mountain turf should break"). But WCB didn't have 50,000 square feet of merchandise to sell off.

In the first days of the sale, the store was crowded as it had not been for years. Carr's was doing a land office business, even though it had frequently offered the same 20 percent off all merchandise in previous sales. "If we had one day like this a month we could go on forever," said Steve as he helped ring us up—for we, too, flew with the circling vultures.

Abashed Wal-Mart customers sweetened their condolences to Beth and Steve with sugar-coated lies of their fidelity. "Oh I've always shopped here," blubbered one woman. "I feel so bad." She patted Beth's arm and said, "I've got to go up to the second floor and see the men's section," unaware that the second floor had been shut down several years earlier.

Beth approaches me. Ever ready with the inappropriate greeting, I burble, "Howya doin'?"

"I've had better weeks," she says in her Nutmeg Hepburn.

"I'm really sorry about the store," I say. "Batavia won't be the same."

She grits her teeth. "Part of me says that Batavia doesn't deserve a store like this," she half-whispers, as if hesitant to speak too loudly the un-American truth that the customer is *not* always right, that sometimes he is a stupid, whinging, greedy bastard. She recounts her string of losing battles as she tried to convince city and county panjandrums to reduce confiscatory property taxes and to locate the unprepossessing new courthouse within walking distance of Main Street merchants.

The air is densely sepulchral over the last weeks; the death rattle is the sound of the movable dress racks and glass display cases being rolled and carried into the whilom gift section, as Carr's condenses, contracts, like a beleaguered band of soldiers drawing in on the last bunker. The mood deepens when Jim Sloper, the longtime vacuum cleaner repairman at the store, dies. Jim was seventy-nine, a farm boy, a crackerjack fixer who loved to tell his World War II stories and who would stare at you for durations sufficient to earn him a Mark on his Permanent Record from Wal-Mart. But at Carr's, Jim was Jim, laboring over a busted hose like Edison at the bench.

The Carr's core mans their stations in best *Titanic* fashion. Marilyn Winegar worked at Carr's for thirty-eight years, beginning in the dress department and ending in children's. Carr's, she says, became "a second home." Rich Doell, the ever-optimistic handyman of twenty years' service, pauses from disassembling a display and responds to the 4,000th commiseration of the last couple of weeks. "If we only had two more years," says Rich, "maybe we could have made it. Maybe downtown will be alive again. Two more years. But we didn't."

It is hard not to see the death of Carr's as the last nail in Main Street's long-shutting coffin. The largest store vacated, no tenant in sight, just as Newberry's has been empty since 1995. Beardsley's is gone. Mancuso Theater is dark (except, I guess, for the light of the

Son). Across Main, the mall is as sparsely populated as the more inclement reaches of the Yukon. My friend Mark Shephard suggests turning Main Street into an interactive prison, as Attica's most notorious fiends could be shipped fifteen miles north to be ogled, prodded, and begged for autographs by morbid tourists. Son of Sam, Mark David Chapman: celebrities living in our little town! Not hippie eggheads like John Gardner but real live certified subjects of *People* magazine! Maybe that fetching eternal blond Diane Sawyer—did she really date Henry Kissinger? How drunk or ambitious or drunkenly ambitious does a girl have to be to engage in foreign affairs with *him?*—could fly in to interview some notorious killer, Live from Batavia! As the New York Lotto ad says: "Hey—ya never know."

Charlotte Conable stops by the store to extend her condolences and buy Estée Lauder perfume. She chats with Steve, and tells a reporter, "I was remembering with him that I had bought my first child's clothing there forty-seven years ago. It's the heart of downtown and certainly a great loss to the community. It will leave a great gap."

With no Gap to take its place, thank heaven for large favors.

The retail hub of Batavia: gone. The old ladies stuck in the two downtown high-rises for the elderly who used to be without cars are now also without Carr's. The walkable center of the city has nowhere to walk to anymore. But did you hear that Bill Paxon's federal prison is hiring? Hey, Batavians—start peeling potatoes for the detained migrant workers. In thirty years you can retire and dribble away your pension check at the Niagara Falls casinos. The American Wet Dream, yanked away in the nickel slots.

The boosters are busy hatching new schemes from the same noggins that produced urban renewal. Expand the airport runway! Bring Lake Ontario water to Batavia, replacing the aqua vitae from good old Tonawanda Creek! (Laying the pipes will require theft via eminent domain on a vast scale, but as good Republicans the city fathers don't mind thievery in the service of Progress.) "It seems that whenever Batavia has made a decision, time proves it to be the wrong decision. Time and time and time again," says Steve.

Also refusing to get with the program and pin on their happy-face buttons are Don and Teresa Doran, whose letter to the *Daily News* was a classic in non-Chamber of Commerce-speak. The Dorans wrote:

> In reply to why Batavians mock out Batavia instead of being proud and trying to make Batavia big, Batavia is funny. What other town would destroy a possible tourist attraction on a continuous basis? Batavia could have been a tourist attraction with all the wonderful history that this town had, but instead every ounce of history is being destroyed by the great community leaders. Why bother publishing flashbacks from the past? It only shows all of us how stupid Batavia is. . . . Books and articles are published about the history of Batavia. People just laugh at that. They say, "If Batavia cared so much about its history, why did they tear everything down?" Do you have an answer? I don't! I am disgusted with Batavia's great plans! They have turned a once beautiful city full of history and industry into a junk city full of modern, no-class buildings and retail stores that benefit no one and they wonder why so many people laugh at Batavia and move away.

Well done, Dorans! (Even if you do laugh at my book.) This is one of the glories of inaffluence: we will never be ruined by yuppies, by gentrifying espresso-sippers, by people who think Molly Ivins is funny. We have the satisfaction of ruining ourselves.

In mid-June I elevate up to the third floor to chat with Steve Carr. Petermumford is with me; he points out that Steve's tie is decorated with life preservers, a nice bit of sartorial happenstance. When I later ask Steve to pose before Nina Mason Booth's portrait of C. L. Carr, Petermumford suggests that he strip to the waist, for after all he's lost his shirt. Cousinly kidding, gallows-style.

Before we discuss the autopsy results, Petermumford leads me through the unseen Carr's, the warehouse and basement and rooftop,

telling stories about each room and portal, every wall crack and fixture. I think of the eighty-six years' worth of oral history that will die
with Petermumford and Steve and Beth and Rich and Marilyn and
all the other wanderers of the coming Carr's diaspora. The manne-
quins are lined up as if for execution on the second floor, in the
former men's wear department. Peter has named them Bliss, Marlene,
Della, Steve. We make the usual lame mannequin jokes. How many
teenage splurts over the years were inspired by the sight of Marlene
in taffeta . . .

Petermumford shows me the vestigial damage from the 1935 fire
that destroyed the neighboring Dellinger Theater on Jackson Street
and filled Carr's with smoke and water. We peer up the shaft of the
ancient elevator, which in my boyhood had an operator to draw closed
the grille. We recall, with relish, eating 50-cent hot dogs and 25-
cent ice-cream cones (Robert Carr used to get pissed off at Petermumford for being too generous with the scoops) and drinking nickel
lemonades at the annual summertime Ye Olde Bargain Days. These
were not Weaver chicken franks and store-brand freezer-burned ice
chunks but dogs with meaty skins and ice cream from Perry's in
nearby Akron.

(Akron, just over the Erie County border, was also home to the
Ford gumball factory. When Lucine and I visited our Akron friend
Lou Nanni, we called upon Lou's Italian grandmother, who lived
across the street from the Ford factory. "Are you hungry?" she asked.
We nodded yes, anticipating some gelato or a Sicilian confection.
Gramma disappeared into the kitchen and returned with a tray loaded
with perhaps twenty skidding gumballs of all colors. God rest her
soul.)

Our cook's tour of Carr's ended, Petermumford and I sit down
with Steve at a table affording a nice view of a flowery still life by
Peter's mother, Virginia Carr Mumford. Over the years I've done more
than a hundred lengthy interviews with the famous, from men who
would be president (usually assholes, e.g., Bill Bradley and Phil
Gramm) to men who dislike finding pubic hairs on cans of Coke

(Clarence Thomas) to men who bum money from me to score crack (Eldridge Cleaver) to men who wrote the American epic (Shelby Foote, who greeted me one afternoon at the door of his mossy Memphis home, hair long and disheveled, wearing ratty pajamas, and said, "Ah wuz jes' fixin' ta go ta thuh whiskey stoah").

Never had I dreaded a talk as I did this one. Kicking a man when he's down is one thing; sticking a tape recorder in his face and asking him to describe the view from the floor is the same thing altogether.

But Steve is well-bred, and he did his manly best to maintain a cheerful mien. He conceded that the store had been "struggling for a long time. But when your name is on the door, there's a responsibility to the history of the business. And the responsibility of being a citizen downtown." History. Citizen. Responsibility. Egads, Steve, these anachronisms are as glaring as Henry W. Clune having a '60s protester bark, "Cheese it, the cops!"

Selling Carr's was never really an option. "Nobody buys a business like this. They just sort of fade into the history books. The real estate sits empty."

I ask Steve whodunit. Urban renewal. Wal-Mart. The obvious suspects. Steve's dad, a progressive businessman, had favored urban renewal: "Our position was that if there was going to be a mall, we were happy that it would be across the street from us." Steve's wife, Beth, the Connecticut Yankee, the pain-in-the-ass daughter-in-law, "was very opposed to urban renewal and said so, but she was not anatomically correct enough to have an opinion." (Like Lucy Gilhooly, Catherine Roth, Marge Cervone: 'twas the women who spoke up to save Batavia from the deaf men of business who destroyed it.)

"Beth is of the opinion," says Steve, assenting, "that with the demolition of downtown Batavia, it lost so much of its character that there was not enough left to hold people, to give them a feeling of community and of belonging." Anchorless, unmoored, Batavians cast about for any port in a storm. How can one be loyal to a place whose structures, whose shape, whose very outline, have simply been erased by its men of substance? (Such substances deserve abuse, puritanical prohibitionists be damned.)

Beth also tried, in vain, to convince Wal-Mart to locate downtown so that at least its overspill might sustain the homegrown merchants. Fat chance. The only company that can put one over on Wal-Mart is its evil twin Kmart, which moved from Eastown Plaza within the city limits to a location just this side of Wal-Mart, so that the faithless shopper must pass the Big K before arriving at Sam Walton's box.

The volk loved it. "Batavia embraces low-price retailers," shrugs Steve. "Every time I turn around something closes and a dollar store opens." (In an inversion of Clarence the Angel's dictum that a bell rings every time an angel gets his wings, a new dollar store also opened as Steve announced the closing of Carr's.)

Old Bob Carr was "progressive": hell, all businessmen are. He cofounded the Progressive Associated Retailers, an organization through which the owners of independent stores in small cities of the Middle Atlantic states might trade tips, trends, tricks of the trade. "All of the stores in PAR are to their town what we are to this town," said Steve in 1990. And then, in the blink of an eye in Bush-Clinton-Bush America, they were gone.

Thirty-four stores have been associated with the Progressive Associated Retailers over the last quarter-century. With the demise of Carr's now there are two: Dunham's in Wellsboro, Pennsylvania, and Friedlander's in Wooster, Ohio. The global economy, it seems, has broken PAR.

It's a dirty job but somebody's got to do it: closing stores, that is. "We've never done this before," said Steve. He met with a man who had "closed a number of my PAR brethren, but he ran out of stores to close and so he closed."

There is a tawdry route to closure, the road most traveled, it seems, but the Carrs did not want a tacky funeral. Steve describes the game: "You pay these people handsomely to come in, you give up control, you buy cameras and VCRs and such and as people shop,

BILL KAUFFMAN

they get points toward these gifts. They also bring in merchandise that is not your normal merchandise—they mark it way up so that they can mark it way down and sell it profitably. It's not of the same quality as what you typically sell; some of it is the dregs left over from the last three or four businesses that they closed. It leaves a bad taste in people's mouths. We decided to handle it ourselves and just go out with our own stuff."

The last day was not July 17, as planned, but two weeks later. The shelves were bare, the workforce had shrunk to three, and instead of the high drama and pathos of an Official Final Day, Steve just shut out the lights, turned the key, and said that was that. The next week he and Beth and the boys left for a month's tour of Europe: a nice Ambersonian touch, I thought, an insouciant up-yours to the Wal-Mart shoppers whose August vacations consist of waterskiing and tossing empty beer cans into the Finger Lakes.

And so died Batavia's Finest Store.

CHAPTER SEVEN

The Other Side of
the Tracks

Working-class Italian Catholic. Middle-class WASP Presbyterian. Multiplying blacks too numerous to confine to lower State Street. White trash mothers slapping unruly children bearing geographic names (Dakota, Sierra) with rolled-up copies of *The National Enquirer*.

Custom forbids Batavians from speaking in mixed company about race, religion, class, or ethnicity. We might offend someone, or accidentally let slip a truth. Yet these categories contain all that spices Batavia. And all that slices and dices Batavia as well. We do not exist without them. Or, rather, we exist only in the way that TV anchors may be said to exist—that is, drained of blood, of color, of anything worthy of being called life.

The tracks of the New York Central railroad bisect Batavia into its north and south sides. The north side was always prosperity and Protestantism; we had our rough neighborhoods, but they were shanty Irish and blond-slattern hillbilly. The south side was Italian and Pole, Tony and Stan, sauce and kielbasa. Carr's department store was on our side of the tracks; Edna's cathouse was on theirs.

Our working men and theirs labored in the same factories—Massey-Harris, Doehler's, Chapin's—but the beefy comradeship stopped when the shift whistle blew. They seldom mixed after hours, except at Batavia Clippers games. No bleacher bum yelled as lustily as a drunken mick, unless it was a half-cocked dago or leather-lunged Polack.

Even within Catholicism, we split along ethnic lines. The Italians built St. Anthony's, the Poles Sacred Heart, and the great Catholic Rest of Us packed St. Joseph's. Those who never could make up their mind on which side of the ethnic fence they belonged joined St. Mary's, which sits along the railroad tracks.

Middle-class Protestants are firm in their conviction (if reticent in its expression) that the Catholics, especially the dagos, ruined Batavia. In *The Resurrection*, John Gardner, that sly old Presbyterian, tied the Italian surge to the knocking down of elm trees. His Welsh-eyed view, from the Putnam Settlement Road:

> What Chandler's father had known about Italians was that they were strangers with strange ways: They talked too loudly, laughed too much, drank wine, made too many friends too soon; they lied, imaginatively, glibly, like grown men with the minds of children; they flirted with one another's wives—even, at times, with a white man's wife (they were never, to Chandler's father, white). When Prohibition came they opened garages and brought in alcohol in the radiators of new cars, and with the money they got they opened pool halls, bowling alleys, roller rinks—strange and obscurely dangerous entertainments. . . . Italians were not quite human. And the proof was simple. If a man named Baker or Brown or Smith walked down South Jackson Street at night he was asking for trouble, and he got it. On the other hand, an Italian could walk wherever he pleased, and *they*, who were civilized, would merely watch him from their windows and, if he loitered, telephone the police. Except that that was an unfair way to put it; the fear of the older Batavians was blind, but not completely unintelligent. Sometimes a loiterer was dangerous, and if a non-Italian did not seem especially

dangerous even when he came up onto your porch, it was because you knew him, or knew his family, or anyway knew exactly where he lived. Nothing on earth could resolve the thing but time, and after a while time had done it.

Time had also robbed the city of its beauty. For the commingling of Italians and whites came at "the cost of the comfortable, narrow old brick street, the trees, the mansions," wrote Gardner. The races mixed, the doves of ethnic amity cooed, and the damned place fell to pieces.

Evidently Gardner was unaware of the almost complete absence of vowel-ending names in the annals of the Batavia Urban Renewal Corporation. After all, by the 1960s our novelist was an expatriate, having taken up permanent residency in University, U.S.A. No doubt he had let his subscription to the *Daily News* lapse. Nevertheless, his linkage of Italian advancement to the retreat of old Batavia is not crack-brained.

The old WASP families disappeared as their college-educated children abandoned Batavia for joyless treeless suburban anonymity. (High average SAT scores! Plenty of golf courses nearby!) As the WASPs left the nest, Batavia's second- and third-generation Italian families prospered. Yes, they stuck indoor porches onto the front of Greek Revival homes, and favored garish Christmas scenes on their lawns (Frosty cradling Baby Jesus while the Wise Men feed Rudolph), but they had arrived.

In my years of exile from Batavia, I forgot just how sharp the rivalry can be between white ethnic groups. To Washingtonians, there is no difference between a Greek-American and a Scots-American, except for the inevitable mustache surmounting the for-mer's upper lip. White is white. All of us achromatics look alike—some are just a whiter shade of pale.

In my Batavia, the Italians were once considered beyond the pale. Not quite white. But now, every day seems to blanch them a little more—to my great disappointment. North-siders no longer rumble with south-siders (in truth, they haven't since the '50s), and, disturbingly, even the Sicilians have cut back on Christmas lights, favoring the simple and monotonous string of white lights (a Martha Stewart Christmas!) over the fat red and blue and green bulbs and blinking Santas of yesteryear. Yet the division between the Italians and everyone else is wide enough to last for another generation, till intermarriage and the continuing flight of the Educated doom us to an endless row of white-lighted December homes.

◻ ◻ ◻

Ellicott Square, at the intersection of Ellicott and Liberty Streets, once formed the locus of the south side. Ange Prospero, historian of the BHS Class of 1947, writes that the Square "provided just about everything for the residents of the south side, mostly inhabited by hardworking Italian and Polish immigrants." The late nineteenth-century tidal wave of immigration that washed over Batavia deposited an estimated 1,500 Poles and 1,500 Italians, mostly Sicilian. Almost all were Catholic, and they reproduced with an admirable profusion. Old Batavia was not beside itself with glee. The *Daily News* commented in 1901, "Those [Italians] who have families here pay their bills, buy groceries, and are an asset to the community. Single young men have to be watched closely."

The closely watched swains eventually found their Marias and Paulinas, who begot the Charleys and Roccos who sired the Kathys and Toms whose Morgans and Taylors think gnocchi is yucky. The fourth-generation Italians and Poles are as American as Pokémon. Why, you can barely get a rise anymore out of your typical flathead with a Polack joke, no matter how risible. So integrated are Poles today that the mildly derisive "Polack" is an anachronism on the order of "jerry" or "bohunk," if not, regrettably, "nigger." (For me, the Polish sense of humor was exemplified by our late neighbor Frank Dziekan, rest his soul, who came home from a day of deer hunting with a mighty buck atop his car and told his horrified toddlers, "Look, kids, Daddy shot Rudolph!")

The swarthy old men on the south side no longer have grapevines from which to transubstantiate wine. Those wrinkled crones not yet reposing in the St. Joe's Cemetery cheat and now drown their pasta in Ragú. And the earth goes around the sun.

Still, the south side remains the south side. Names end in vowels, the decibel level is higher, faithful Ninas and Ninos work the garlicy booths at the St. Anthony's lawn fete each July. The Italianness may be etiolated, but it ain't bleached out yet. And serving as a constant reminder of South Side Past is Vincenzo Del Plato's *Ellicott Square Mural.* This is the finest piece of public art I have ever seen, a painting that makes grown men and women cry. (Yes, yes, I know, they weep at Richard Serra, too, but not for the same reason.)

Del Plato's mural covers the eastern side of Willie's Barbecue, né Gioa's Drugs, which as late as the '60s advertised its pharmacopic wares in Polish and Italian. This is ground zero of Batavia Italia. Fifty years ago, Gardners and Kauffmans ventured this far southward at their own risk. "You had to fight your way back to the north side," says my dad, a jock.

The only danger a Kauffman faces today on Ellicott Square is choking on the exhaust fumes, but even from the windows of four-wheeled death traps one can see Vinny's mural, and very often Vinny himself, the Diego (*not* Dago) Rivera of Ellicott Square.

I meet Vinny for breakfast at his hangout, a black and white diner across the street from Willie's called the Pokadot. Painted in polkadots, the joint would be called funky if Batavia had yuppies. But we don't, so most non-south-side Italians call it a dive. Vinny and his brothers—Carmen, Joe, and Mookie—meet for a weekly 11 A.M. Saturday breakfast. Rat's-nest-haired Vinny arrives late, wearing a beret and paint-splattered sweats.

"He's an artist," Joe says, rolling his eyes. In fact, he is Artist-in-Residence at the Pokadot. A Del Plato bananas-and-apples still life hangs over the unisex toilet, though a philistine has attached a supermarket price sticker to one of the bananas.

I ask Vinny, who has painted murals up and down Ellicott Street, about his masterwork. "I looked at that wall for a long time," he says—a lifetime, in fact. Vinny Del Plato grew up on Hutchins Street, two blocks from Gioa's Drugs; he still lives in the Del Plato homestead with brother Joe.

The mural depicts "heaven on earth," says Vinny, a St. Anthony's boy who regularly confesses but no longer attends mass. In his creation, cherubim surround the Italian folk dancers who swirl around an all-star Batavia band as south-siders dead and alive dine streetside, flanked by Vincenzo the artist and Father Kirby of St. Anthony's, the kindly shepherd.

The seventy or so subjects are not the carefully apportioned p.c. blanks of your standard urban mural, which usually features a (characterless) black, a (characterless) Latino, a (characterless) Asian, and maybe a (characterless) white, if the artist has room. No, these are specific men and women: Louie Fanara the barber and Mary Tenebruso the matriarch, Roxy Caccamise the accordionist and Sam Baudanza the cop. Vinny reels off the names, all evocatively Batavian: Mancuso, Riccobono, Perkowski, DiFilippo, Ferrando, Swase, Berardini, Tiede, Zinni, Pellegrino, Marcello, Puccio.

There's Tom Gullo the shoe repairman, who would spend half a day resoling my shoes and hand me a bill for $2.45. Two black kids seem to interrupt the Italianness of the mural, but in fact they deepen and extend it: no bloodless multicult tokens, they are the mixed race great-grandchildren of the diners. "Some Italians were pissed off that I put them in," says the artist.

Vinny points out that the midget mulattoes are not the only revelers without the boot stamped on their faces. "Sam and Betty Pontillo," the first family of Batavia pizza, "told me, 'Why don't ya put Edna in there?'" recalls Vinny, whose studio was in Edna's erstwhile whorehouse on Jackson Street. "Okay, you want Edna? Then you're gonna be sittin' at the table with her." Which they are.

As he painted the mural in 1998, Vinny's wall became the talk of the south side. People came to him requesting that relatives join the party. A bereaved father in tears appeared; his son is now the smiling waiter holding a bottle of wine. Joe "Brownie" La Russa (who took the photo-finish pictures at the Batavia Downs harness-racing track) became the band's trombonist. "He lived long enough to see it," says Vinny. "His sister and his niece came around almost daily checking it out. They drove him by to see the mural and he cried." The mural has that effect on people: last year, on the anniversary of south-sider Sam Dorsey's death, his widow laid flowers in front of his image.

Vinny's painting has joined St. Anthony's Roman Catholic Church, the St. Nick's social club, and the Paolo Busti Society as the cornerstones of what remains of Italo-Batavian culture. (The Paolo Busti Society takes its name from the Milan-born Dutch banker who served as the Philadelphia-based general agent for the Holland Land Company, the absentee owners that sold off western New York.)

I tell Vinny that he is "Batavia's Artist." He is pleased with the sobriquet, though as a good south-sider he will be forever at war with Those Who Run Things. He itemizes his complaints: "I did a drawing of the Muckdog logo—half dog, half baseball player—but it wasn't even considered. They selected the logo before the deadline." He adds that the city's cultural organizations "never invited me to do a workshop. Pissed me off. Now if they invite me I won't do it."

As with the other south-side Italians, Vinny cannot always disagree agreeably. In the course of a letter to the *Daily News* arguing that Batavia should switch from the city-manager system to an elected mayor (he is absolutely right), Vinny sneers that John Hodgins is incapable of "rendering the human form," a cheap shot at our outstanding landscape artist. But then John is a north-side Republican, a business owner, a county legislator. He lives on the right side of the railroad tracks that still divide the town.

And so we are left with Vincenzo and his mural, conjuring the spirits of all those plump St. Joseph's bread-baking Italian ladies, the smooth-talking Louies and tongue-tied musicians, Father Kirby murmuring the Confession of Faith. The mural takes my breath away: the Resurrection, as performed by Mad Vinny.

His last words at our breakfast gnaw at me. I ask him about growing old in Batavia, eating a lifetime of eggs over easy at the Pokadot, painting the faces of his boyhood. "If I stay healthy, I'll graduate this place," he says. "That's what Roy Mason did."

True. In retirement, our best-known native painter went west, to La Jolla, where he produced uninspired seascapes of the sort that might hang in the Mai Tai Room at Don the Beachcomber's. Vinny dreams of painting in Italy, a Michelangelo in a land that already had one. We never are satisfied with where we are, are we?

◻ ◻ ◻

Vinny became Vincenzo once the oil splashed the canvas. Similarly, our Genesee Symphony Orchestra conductor Raffaele Livio Ponti was once plain old Ralph. Art elevates, don't you know, and these fore-name refinements seem perfectly natural—unlike some surname surgeries.

For instance, Batavia's hero in the Second World War was Captain Eddie York, a leader of the legendary Jimmy Doolittle's April 1942 air raid against Japan, the first direct assault on Tojo's homeland. Eddie was the son not of Mr. and Mrs. Frederick York of Ellicott Avenue but of Mr. and Mrs. Ignacy Cichowski of 101 Harvester Avenue. He grew up just down the street from the almost Pole-less Batavia Cemetery and the Massey-Harris plant in which Ignacy worked as a molder.

Eddie is a classic case of the deracinating effect of the empire's military. The precocious Pole was graduated from Batavia High School at age fifteen. He joined the army and was plucked from the grunt ranks and sent to West Point. He played football for the Black Knights of the Hudson and bid good-bye to the golabki eaters of Harvester Avenue.

Eddie Cichowski was graduated from West Point in 1938. His anglicized doppelganger, Eddie York, earned the Distinguished Service Cross as third in command of the daring raid on the Nipponese. Eddie's parents are pictured in a *Daily News* article of May 20, 1942, touching a photograph of their son the hero, the absurdly named Mr. York, his new cognomen evidently carrying a cachet among the officer class that Cichowski lacked.

Eddie spent forty postwar years in Europe and living on the reservations known as U.S. military bases—anywhere but south-side Batavia. His remains are in San Antonio. Those of his brother, the plumber Matt Cichowski, whose "Proud Parents" never smiled shyly over his picture in the newspaper, but who never dishonored Ignacy and Tekla by scrapping their name, are inhumed in the St. Joseph's cemetery on Harvester Avenue. So who was the success?

Pronunciation, not dissimulation, cleaves the Marcheses, one of Batavia's best-liked Italian families. Bob Marchese (Mar-kay-zee) is our dentist. Along with our lawyer Tom Williams, Doctor Bob is an outstanding example in the case for living in your hometown.

You see, Bob and Tom were two of the brightest kids in the class behind me. ("Kids." I'll be like my dad, remembering dead seventy-five-year-olds from the sandlot and calling them "kids.") Were I a rootless professional in some nameless burg, I would know nothing of the backgrounds of the men who drill my teeth and draw my will. I would choose dentist and lawyer and butcher and baker and candlestick maker by sortilege, hoping against hope that I didn't draw a fraud. After all, as the old gag goes, what do you call the cretin who ranks last in his graduating class at medical school? Doctor.

In my town, I know the sharp tacks and the lunkheads, the pure-hearts and the crooks. Dr. Bob yanks my wisdom teeth because over the long decades I have known him to be wise. Tom Williams, our lawyer, I know well to be the Atticus Finch of Batavia. Tom is a wisecracking liberal who was graduated from Columbia Law School and came home to practice with his dad in Williams and Williams, taking clients he knows cannot pay, consistently undercharging for mortgages, and throwing in wills gratis to the everlasting chagrin (and secret pride) of his wonderful wife, Barb Miller.

As far as I know there are no variant pronunciations of Williams, but as I mentioned, the Marchese branches do divide over matters pronunciatory. In my boyhood all Marcheses went by "Mar-cheese," until one wing of the family undertook a citywide campaign to re-educate Batavians to say "Mark-Kay-Zee," with its aristocratic air. Batavians being Batavians, ever on the lookout for "uppityness," a Resistance developed. Now the town is split between compliant Mar-Kay-Zee sayers and indurated crabs who pronounce it "Mar-Cheesy."

Dr. Bob is a Mar-Kay-Zee, but I never can get used to it. (And now a branch of the German hardware-store family named Buchholtz— "Buck-Holtz" since time immemorial, or 1930 anyway—has taken to calling itself "Boo-Holtz." This, I gather, is not an homage to the South Carolina football coach.)

The wretched theme song of the tavernous TV comedy *Cheers* contained a sage line about wanting to go where everybody knows your name—which is emphatically *not* to a chain of fern-bar restaurants decorated with the grisly visage of Ted Danson. Yet the sentiment is honest and true. It explains, I think, much of the appeal of small-town life. In Batavia, people do know your name—even if they mispronounce it.

Let me illustrate. In the midst of writing this chapter came a typical Batavia day; perhaps a brief recapitulation will explain why I could not live elsewhere. I drove the five miles from Elba to My Hometown, stopping first at Bob Youll's Vac Shop on Ellicott Street. Bob gave our late '60s avocado vacuum cleaner the once-over, slipped on a new belt, pronounced it fit and ready for another 20,000 linty miles, and charged me the grand total of two dollars.

Then it was off to the Richmond Memorial Library, where I spent an intoxicating fifteen minutes chatting with Dorothy Coughlin, for many decades the adored English teacher and anchor of Elba Central School. (Middle-aged men who have not cracked a book since stepping out of school and onto the muck still recite Burns and Whittier and speak of Miss Coughlin with the reverence reserved for saints.) Miss Coughlin tells me a few stories of Irish-Catholic farm life in the '30s and offers kindhearted advice on the book, reminding me that even people who do dreadful things have moments of peace, of twilight longing, of deserved love.

From the Richmond I'm off to the county history department, housed in the Henry Homelius–designed, turret-guarded 1885 firehouse. I park under the enormous watertower whose construction was superintended by my distant uncle Dan Kauffman. Sue Conklin and Ellen Bachorski direct me to the files I seek, and when I bring my batch of off-center Xeroxes to them Sue says, "No charge today." I drive past the poet John Yates's home, a tenderly restored Gothic, and past Dwyer Stadium and MacArthur Park, where at eventide I will take Gretel swimming in the wading pool of my youth. After our dip we will hunt in the grass beyond the right-field wall for batting-practice official NYP League home runs (we always find one or two). Then we will attend the Muckdogs game, where we sit among friends, old and new, in the third-base bleachers barely a block from the Kauffman homestead. This is my place, and whatever I might say about it, however caustic or corrosive my pen, I love it and will forever.

◻ ◻ ◻

The Ku Klux Klan surged briefly in the Batavia of the 1920s, as it resurged in points south. Its target was not blacks, for Batavia was monochromatic, but Catholics, specifically Italians.

The Kluxers tended to be rural Protestants, Grangers and small farmers, who had heard one "meenga fotch" too many on Batavia streets. Their world was disappearing 'neath a blizzard of rosary beads. Incense incensed them. But I refuse to draw down my meager reservoir of smug moral superiority to condemn these confused and basically harmless men who chalked their crosses outside my ancestors' church. These weren't southern night riders lynching black men under the magnolia tree. Our Klansmen were hardscrabble farmers trying pathetically (and nonviolently) to repel the pope's legions.

Charles Buxton, resident of an apartment over a Main Street storefront, defended the Triple K in a 1922 letter to the *Daily News*: "Personally, I think that non-Catholic, non-Jewish, non-negro, and, I might add, non-bootlegger, gambler and woman-chaser would be the best way to describe the order." And it didn't abominate *all* nonwhites. Significantly, the musical entertainment for a 1924 gathering of 5,000 Klansmen at the Genesee County fairgrounds was provided in part by members of the Tonawanda Seneca Indian band. When the Klan said that it represented "native Americans," it meant it.

In 1923, the men of St. Joseph's, my parish and that of my parents and grandparents and great-grandparents, faced down 2,000 Klan marchers as they tried to parade past the church. It was a richly mythopoeic moment—at least in folklore, for documentation eludes me. How I want it to be so: to have Garraghan men, my Irish forebears, standing stalwart and silent as the white hoods beat a cowardly retreat. We're all entitled to a legend or two, aren't we?

St. Joseph's was the first Catholic church in Batavia and was for years the most prominent. Its first mass was said on Easter Sunday 1849. Demonstrating the money-dunning prowess for which the men of St. Joe's would become famous, parishioners raised $45,000 toward the construction of a new church in 1864. Among the generous donors was our railroad baron, Dean Richmond. So grateful were the humble flock of St. Joe's that a century later we located our parking lot where Dean's home had stood. Served the old Episcopalian right.

You will forgive me, I know, if I skip one hundred years of novenas and First Communions and weddings and extreme unctions: the daily acts that make holy a church, and whole a community. For in 1960, a new padre swaggered into town. Father (later Monsignor) Francis Schwartz was a tough German kid from Buffalo. How my jaw dropped the first time I heard him say "son of a bitch." A priest, for God's sake!

Schwartz took over the pastorate of St. Joe's from the beloved Father T. Bernard Kelly. Father Kelly's winsomeness may be gleaned from this tale by his nephew, Paul Gerace: "He was not known for being the best driver. Nor was Monsignor Kirby [of St. Anthony's and Vincenzo Del Plato's mural] known for his driving. We lived on Summit Street, and one day I was out in the yard and looked up to see a car coming down Summit on the wrong side of the road. Then I saw another car heading north from St. Joseph's rectory. But it was all right, because he was also on the wrong side of the road. There was Monsignor Kirby coming from Genesee Memorial Hospital and my uncle heading for the hospital, and they passed—each driving on the [wrong] side of the road."

Father Schwartz would have hogged the whole damned road to himself. He was hale, hearty, and manly. Schwartz was no milksop priest. Some revered him for his strength. Others despised him for his conspicuous Cadillac-driving failure to keep his vow of poverty. Pencil me in as one of the few undecideds.

Father Schwartz was as enthusiastic about eradicating the old Batavia as was the city's Protestant leadership. In 1963, the Schwartz-era St. Joe's demolished its school and convent to make room for a parking lot. The new school and convent were constructed on land donated by a reclusive Catholic pianist named Monica Dailey, who left everything she owned to the church—whereupon the church tore down everything she owned. Ashes to ashes, dust to bank account.

Schwartzie also chaired the Batavia Housing Authority, which spent federal monies to build ugly tenements for poor people who had heretofore lived in the walkups and nineteenth-century apartments destroyed by urban renewal. The priest, like the prototypical Batavia businessman, was nothing if not progressive.

The Dailey Demolition was the prelude to the consuming conflagration of my youth, the night they burned old St. Joe's down.

By the late '60s, Father Schwartz had tired of the Civil War–era church, whose stained glass and flickering votive candles and magnificent altar fairly obligated a priest to say hour-long masses, else he wasn't really doing his job. (Father Schwartz was a devout believer in the half-hour mass, which is why he was a Kauffman family favorite.) So the shepherd of St. Joe's convinced his flock to raze the church of their fathers and build a boxy new worship center in the spirit(lessness) of Vatican II. It was a building better suited to use as a wholesale club selling paper towels and Nabisco products at bulk discounts.

As the new St. Joe's went up, three fires, their origins suspicious to varying degrees, broke out over a span of six months in the soon-to-be-desanctified St. Joe's. The final and most dubious fire, on a July evening in 1970, finished off the old church.

The Batavia Trojans were home that night, so from the grandstand our family watched the flames brighten the night. We cut out around the seventh-inning stretch in order to bear witness as one world ended in fire—so conveniently for St. Joe's, which was saved demolition costs—and another was born in the icy new warehouse that stole the name of St. Joseph's.

As a good—well, middling—Catholic boy, I feel the cinch of a phantom heart attack as I write these irreverent lines. But isn't truth a defense even in heresy trials? We remain the largest parish in Batavia—1,400 families and falling—but I'll be damned (I probably am already) if the Holy Spirit resides therein.

◻ ◻ ◻

I am blessed with a mongrel lineage—Irish Catholic, German Lutheran, English Baptist, Italian Catholic—and thus am sympathetic to all sides in Batavia's ethno-religious wars. Yet on occasion I am struck—like a discus to the temple of a hapless track official—with the realization of Catholicism's utter irrelevance to

Batavia's long slow procession into nothingness. Middle-class Protestants built Batavia, they supplied its pith and brain, its wealth and
culture and vitality, and then they killed it. As a Catholic, I'm like
the ineffectual lover in the Lou Reed song. I am just a waterboy. The
real game ain't over here.

The old Italian and Irish ladies worry their beads and beseech
their idols while the men sell tickets to the cars raffled off every
summer at the church lawn fetes. And they were and are as powerless
to stop the college-degreed Protestants from murdering Batavia as I
was to keep Niagara Mohawk from clear-cutting our trees. I'm just
the waterboy.

My Grandfather Kauffman, a legendarily kind man and fiery
populist who understood full well the utter futility of his politics, was
ahead of me on this, as on everything. "I was in the back," Grandpa
explained with an amused smile whenever we told him that we hadn't
seen him in church that morning. Think of all those Irish colleens
and Italian fireballs coaxing halfhearted conversions, and their
apostate husbands drifting off, finally mumbling a simple Hail me-
a-cab Mary.

Grandpa ran for city council on the Democratic ticket, which
outside the south side is a ticket to perdition. He was a north-side
working-class Democrat who'd have been as out of place in today's
race- and gender-obsessed national Democratic Party as he would
be among the Fortune 500 waterboys of the GOP. I guess he just
wasn't made for these times.

I have a Doehler factory ID button bearing Grandpa's mug
shot: he looks like Jimmy Stewart, if Jimmy had gone onto the shop
floor in Indiana, Pennsylvania, instead of to architecture class at
Princeton.

As recently as 1980, 45 percent of Batavia's workforce was
employed in manufacturing, at Doehler and Graham and Chapin and
other well-paying plants. By 2000, the figure was less than half that
and falling. The service sector had zoomed from 23 percent of the

workforce in 1980 to almost half come the millennium. The living wage provided by the likes of Doehler to men like Grandpa Kauffman has gone the way of the Latin Mass; the majority of factory jobs in today's Batavia are low wage, no benefits, and nonunion.

Which leads us to class, the great unmentionable in the America in which anyone whose father was a U.S. senator can grow up to be president.

I have a grim story—how I wish it was a Grimm's fairy tale— about class. It has no moral, no lesson; nothing good can be taken from it. But it really happened. In Batavia.

Lyndon Duane Goodell—the middle name is the signifier; middle-class mamas don't dub their babies Duane or Darrell—was a dimwitted metalhead named, no doubt, for the man who was president of the United States at his nativity. My boy's gonna grow up to be . . .

Goodell was a precocious boozer, a bit of a punk but more a loser than a malicious kid. He quit BHS at sixteen. Later an acquaintance told the *Daily News*, "He wasn't smart. He couldn't keep up with his peers in class, and he was no good in sports." While locked up for a petty crime in the county jail, Goodell forever earned the enmity of the local constabulary when, in a Keystone Kops escape attempt, he crawled through a false ceiling and promptly fell onto the chief deputy's desk. He got up, dusted himself off, and jumped out the window. He was caught the next day, drinking gin in Mac-Arthur Park.

Out of jail, on a June day in 1987, Goodell hooked up with the daughter of a far more affluent Buffalo family. (True love breaks through class lines, à la Leo DiCaprio and Kate Winslet aboard that doomed ocean liner. . . .) He got roaring drunk in a suburban Buffalo mall parking lot, and drove her red Grand Prix (window sign: "I brake for hallucinations") back to Genesee County. Numerous drivers reported that a car was weaving dangerously in and out of traffic. A sheriff gave pursuit, but too late: Goodell's car collided head-on with a driver's-ed vehicle, killing three Pembroke students and their teacher. The dead were good kids, honor students—anti-Goodells; they included the president of the school chapter of Students Against Drunk Driving.

The scene of the crime was carnage and chaos. An almost empty fifth of Jack Daniels was stashed under the front seat. It was impossible to tell for certain whether Goodell or the girl had been driving the car, though the alignment of the bodies suggested that it was the boy. In any event, Goodell was in a coma from which doctors did not expect him to revive. The girl, though in critical condition, appeared likely to recover. The sheriff from whose jail the young drunk had escaped arrested Goodell; he was charged with manslaughter, though it was assumed he would never live to stand trial.

Goodell survived. He was tried and convicted, despite his public defender's claim that he was *not driving the car.* The families of the dead would not, and will not, have anything of it: they burned with an almost pure hatred of Goodell, and who can blame them? Kate Winslet—granted immunity, never even given a blood alcohol test—walked away unpunished, in this life at least. In the years since, it became known that a woman claiming to be an eyewitness told sheriffs that a girl was driving the murder weapon. This woman, who had a reputation for unreliability, went to her grave protesting that Goodell's lead foot was not on the pedal. I have friends in Batavia law enforcement who suspect she was right. But I have more friends who say that she was nuts, and that Goodell was the murderer.

I don't know if this was a miscarriage of justice or not, except for the dead girls and their teacher. There was nothing good about Lyndon Duane Goodell. He was headed for the Loserville of petty larcenies and DWI arrests. His mother's illusion aside, he was not White House–bound. Goodell was released from Attica Prison in December 1999, after serving more than twelve years. He continues to maintain his innocence and refuses to so much as apologize to the families of the dead.

No matter. The girls and the driving instructor are dead. The sheriff resigned shortly thereafter, disputing accounts that a guilty conscience over the railroading of Lyndon Goodell impelled his retirement. I believe him. He remains active in civic affairs, and did yeoman's work in raising funds for the reconstruction of Dwyer Stadium.

I get queasy even typing the name Lyndon Goodell. How I wish he and his crime could be erased. As was his family home. The Goodells' run-down place on West Main Street, on the banks of the Tonawanda—how often must the families of those girls have wished that young Lyndon had splashed unsupervised in the muddy creek, sinking as the world looked the other way?—was torn down recently to make a parking lot for Oliver's Candies, Batavia's chocolate contribution to the national cuisine. (Jackie Gleason was a customer.) The Oliver's lot is backed by a ten-foot-high white picket fence along which John Hodgins has painted a series of seasonal images—hearts for Valentine's Day, bunnies for Easter, pumpkins for Halloween, Santa for Christmas. This was one Batavia demolition that I did not mourn.

❒ ❒ ❒

One of the most striking examples of the poisonous fallout of mass culture came from a conversation I had in the mid-'90s with a friend of mine, a Batavia cop. He told me of an encounter he'd had with a couple of boisterous, but by no means bad, black kids.

"We the boyz in the hood," they told him. Their hood encompassed perhaps five contiguous houses on lower State Street. "White man's tryin' to wipe us out."

My friend, the white cop, asked them to explain.

"There's a liquor store on every corner, and a gun store, too. That ain't no accident. Whites want us to get drunk and shoot each other."

My friend was perplexed. There's only one liquor store downtown; its clientele, like Batavia's population, is overwhelmingly white. Our gun shop is on the city's outskirts, and it caters to sportsmen and collectors. It sells Baker Black Beauties and Winchester hunting rifles, not cheap handguns.

Besides, we have a murder seldom more than once every two or three years—and these are usually committed by boozed-up, jealous, poor, and very white ex-husbands or boyfriends. I can think of only one black man arrested for murder in the last decade. He killed a white bum who had attacked his brother, and because public sympathy ran so strongly in his favor he was let off with a rap on the knuckles.

So the picture that these kids on State Street had drawn for the policeman bore no resemblance whatsoever to life as it was actually lived in Batavia, New York, circa 1995. God knows that Batavia's blacks have legitimate grievances (as do the elderly whites on lower State who undergo daily aural assaults in the lexicon of muthafuckery). But a white plot hatched by the Rotary and Kiwanis Clubs to lead Afro-Batavians into intoxicated fratricide is not among them.

It turns out that these kids had merely recited, almost verbatim, the hero's sermon in John Singleton's film *Boyz N the Hood*. Singleton's violent South Central Los Angeles block had been transplanted to Batavia. Which might have been cute—like Vietnamese refugees in 1982 Iowa speaking Valley Girl—had it not provided these young men with a sham view of their world. Such are the delusions induced in young and old, black and white, by masscult, which never reflects the realities of the life of Batavia. (The antidote, I would argue, is not so much political—though there are various localist measures that would help, for instance smashing the communications oligopolies—as it is personal and communal, a small but meaningful example being our attempt to revive our shaggy Mr. Gardner.)

I should add that my friend, a superb officer, is one of the last homeboy cops. Ed Kauffmans no longer walk the beat, thanks to the civil service exams so fetishized in our Land of the Free and Home of the Standardized Test. The recent hires in the Batavia Police Department tend to be outsiders, Buffalo pals who never cut a Batavia sucker an even break, and who entertain those listening to police scanners with their frequent laments of "I'm lost" and "Where is Thorpe Street?" We are in precisely the same situation as those urban blacks whose streets are patrolled by suburban micks who disparage them as no-good scrofulous niggers. We'll never realize it, of course—nor will the bruthas. Epiphanies tend to occur to those on their way out, like the Branch Davidians who unrolled a banner reading "Rodney King: We Understand"—and we all know what happened to that merry band of religious dissenters. They fought the law and the law won. (That once-great Bobby Fuller Four/Clash tune was ruined for me when I learned that it was written by the same guy who penned the theme to *The Mary Tyler Moore Show.* Who can turn the world on with her smile . . . ?)

In matters black and white, I understand perfectly well the story I am supposed to tell in Imperial America, a yarn that has all the sophistication of an *ABC Afterschool Special.* The formula goes like this: a noble Sidney Poitier Negro, taciturn and dignified, moves to The Small Town. Kids bust his windows, his daughter is hassled at school, he is threatened—"Y'all betta go back whar ya came from"—by menacing thugs speaking in improbable southern cracker accents. I have seen this movie a thousand times—my cheeks are wetted every time we watch *To Kill a Mockingbird.* But it don't play in Batavia. No lynch mobs, no Tom Robinsons, just . . . a mess.

The black population in Batavia has multiplied exponentially over the last thirty years, from a fraction of 1 percent in my boyhood to 5.4 percent in the 2000 census. Batavia's dozen or so Jewish families had always been part of us while remaining somehow separate. The same was true of such old black families as the Thomases, whose father, William, a car salesman, was elected to the school board in 1973, and whose sons Bill and Greg, boon companions of my youth, starred on the Blue Devils' five.

The high school basketball team, heretofore a basket case, is the one unalloyed success story of biracial Batavia. The black influx has recomplected the Blue Devils, now commonly referred to sub rosa as the Globetrotters. In 1998, Batavia won the Section V Class B championship, a first for our air-ball town.

The coach, the mighty resuscitator of BHS basketball, is Bud Brasky, who graduated with me in the Class of '77. Bud, born Myron, is the latest in a line of fine Batavia athletes named Myron Brasky, stalwarts of the Polish Falcons' athletic teams. Bud has named his boys Alex, Adam, and Jake, to his father Myron's dismay, but he has made up for the absence of Myron IV by living just one street away from his folks, in the Polish strip of the south side.

Bud was not my buddy. He was a jock in high school, though a friendly enough fellow, certainly not a malevolent let's-make-fun-of-the-retards brute. When I called him to chat about his team, he mistook me for my brother, Mike, an excellent athlete, as all Kauffmans but I had been. As for me, I am the waterboy. . . .

I ask Bud if he dreamed as a child of someday coaching the Blue Devils. "To be honest, I did. As far back as junior high this is what I wanted to be." He is thus that rarest of modern Batavians: the right man for the right job. He is also a critical link between Batavias: he connects the dago-Polack past with the far less numerous new Batavians of duskier hue.

"The beauty of sports" is that it brings black and white together, says Bud, and before the maudlin strains of "Ebony and Ivory" waft over the wires I realize for about the eighty-fourth time that this cliché is true. "These kids ride in each other's cars, hang out together," he says. I think of the 1930s photos of Batavia High teams, the years in which Italian names started appearing regularly.

At midcentury, the symbol of the Italian arrival was Batavia High football coach Danny Van Detta, a hard-nosed ass-kicker whose teams were among the state's finest. Upon his death, the stadium, formerly named for the Woodwards, the Jell-O magnates of nearby Le Roy, was rechristened Van Detta Stadium. 'Tis a plausible reverie to imagine Brasky Fieldhouse dedicated in 2030; as for the coming of our black Van Detta . . . who knows?

In the meantime, I watch the championship game of the Batavia Lions Club tournament, which pits Batavia against Notre Dame. Four of the starting five for the Blue Devils are black; the fifth regular starter is spending the night in jail for stealing a necklace. (Bud tells me that the scholar-athlete "didn't steal it—he was at the scene.")

Necklace stealing. Team introductions accompanied by the urban thump of rap music. Players who can actually dunk the ball.

Is this really my school? Like most Americans, I used to root for the basketball team with the most white guys. I realize that such simple truths are simply unsayable in the land of the free, but what the hell—and I do have an addendum. As an America Firster, I deplore the NBA's importation of Serbs, Croats, and other giraffe-ish Slavs in a fairly bald attempt to put racist white fannies in the seats and on the couches, so in pro ball, the reverse obtains: I generally pull for the blacker team. That is, unless its base is Los Angeles or New York City, which must be held in a state of perpetual execration. But this is the Lions Tournament, not a Serb in sight, and I pull for Batavia because, well, I am a Batavian, and so are they now. Plus, I have never much liked the prototypical Notre Damer: a cocky Italian with his hair parted in the middle.

One week later, the arrestee is back in the starting lineup. Batavia plays to win, even though we lose at everything not involving a ball. The team's other black star, Ben, is to the necklace stealer as Booker T. Washington is to Sonny Liston. The son of greatly respected parents, he will go to Oswego State to play ball and major in computer science. If only Batavia knew how to keep its Bens.

◻ ◻ ◻

In the championship season of 1997–1998, Lucine, longtime JV boys' and girls' tennis coach at BHS, was cajoled into coaching the basketball cheerleaders. Sports-mad Batavia High had just imposed a truly draconian eligibility policy upon athletes—fail two grades in a marking period and you were given a *stiff warning*—and the young scholars were dropping like flies in a tee-ball game. Lucine was left with a squad of seven plucky, admirable, and athletic girls whose composite pigmentation was far darker than any I had remembered at BHS.

A Southern California girl who grew up in the endless summer of surf and rock and roll bars, Lucine is somewhere this side of prudish, but she nixed the lewd belly-shaking and pelvis-pushing that passes for high school cheerleading today. (The Tennessee poet Donald Davidson, the one contributor to the 1930 agrarian manifesto *I'll Take My Stand* who remained unalterably loyal to the old creed—including its racial caste system—thought cheerleading a lubricious symbol of the decline of southern womanhood. Consider that Senator Trent Lott was a cheerleader at Ole Miss, and ask yourself if crusty old Davidson wasn't right.)

Subsequent cheerleader coaches have not all shared Lucine's modesty. At one Batavia Lions Club Christmas Basketball Tournament, Mike Sheehan and I laughed our asses off as two gymnastic Batavia cheerleaders, pigtails bobbing, flipped their way across the basketball floor to the thumping of AC/DC's "You Shook Me All Night Long." To the deaf fan, this presents such a homey small-town tableau: the pretty tomboy next door is doing cartwheels! Those of us with functioning auditory systems gaze upon this Americana with a soundtrack, as Satan's favorite metalheads testify to the joy of being headlocked between a pair of good old American thighs.

And yet one January night in the BHS gym I saw a dream walking. A giggly and beaming black girl sang the national anthem, con brio. She and her friends were decked out in blue and white "BHS: The Pride Is Alive" T-shirts. The team got off to a terrific start, passing and setting picks like a quintet of black Bob Cousys, and as the girls thrust their fists into the air, chanting "BHS! BHS! BHS!" as generations past have done, I felt a tickling at the corner of my eye. Like the Van Dettas and Braskys of decades ago, these girls had become Batavians through sport.

I closed my eyes and whispered, "Maybe there's hope, maybe there's hope, maybe there's hope. . . ."

CHAPTER EIGHT

. . . And Here I'll Stay

The best view in Batavia is from the Blind School. I don't mint these incongruities, I just report 'em.

The New York State School for the Blind was authorized by the state legislature in 1865, after four years of fratricidal cannon blast and bullet strike had hollowed sockets and nullified eyes that once had been bright with the light of God's creation. War—what is it good for, eh? In 1866, a site-selection committee chose fifty acres of hilltop land in Batavia, one-third of whose cost was donated by Dean Richmond. (And in return the Blind School sits on Richmond Avenue.)

The school opened in 1868. Blind veterans of the War Between the States, Abraham Lincoln's Sightless Legions, were given preference in postbellum admissions. Drummer boys and lackbeard Union soldiers learned broom making, rug weaving, and other skills for which ocular keenness is not a requisite. One rather doubts they wove and braided in cheerful darkness, consoled by the knowledge that before their legs were amputated they had trampled out the vintage where the grapes of wrath were stored.

The Blind School, as it is colloquially known, eventually became "in the town but not of the town," to quote our percipient historian Miss McEvoy. We Batavians grew up on streets filled with blind children navigating with pointer sticks. They walked among us, buying penny candy at Lambert's and giggling over the usual juvenilia.

I think back and regret never once having engaged one of these blind temporary Batavians in conversation, yet in my defense, opportunities for exchange with the blind were severely limited.

The school was an island unto itself; until the 1950s, green-thumbed employees even cultivated a huge garden which sustained the residents of this K–12 school for sightless New Yorkers aged five to twenty-one. Most of its students were boarders who hailed from elsewhere in the Empire State. The curriculum was in many respects indistinguishable from that of Batavia High, as students studied grammar, arithmetic, and geography. They played in a dance band, took piano lessons, sang in a choir, acted in a school play (not *Wait Until Dark*), and even fielded a wrestling team, which grappled gamely against the sighted teams of Genesee County.

Henry Emmans, whose wife, Ann, is at the ivories whenever culture erupts in Batavia, be it the disastrous invasion of Stephen Sondheim or the canorous tones of "The Old Rugged Cross" at funerals, wrote a history of the Blind School for its 100th anniversary in 1967–1968.

Henry emphasized the musical qualities of the school, as did its first superintendent, Dr. Asa Lord, who steered the more capable early graduates toward the worthy vocation of piano tuning. Under the aptly named Lord, the school was energetically Christian, for as the *Progressive Batavian* (was there any other kind?) reported in 1870, "the religious experience of these blind people, shut out from the world, seems to be unusually deep and strong." That may well still be true, but today the Bible has been purged from the Blind School as thoroughly as it has been from the public schools of the United States and Iran.

In recent times, John and Helen Grapka, charter members of the Genesee Symphony Orchestra, taught Blind School students every sort of instrument: piano, oboe, clarinet, trumpet, strings. "Everything had to be memorized," said John. "They're hams, regular hams, I tell you."

Or at least they used to be. By the 1980s, blind children lacking any other handicap were "mainstreamed" into their local public school systems. Admission to the Blind School became a kind of reverse lottery in which only the most luckless and severely disabled might win: students must not merely be blind but must also be handicapped by cerebral palsy, retardation, autism, or any of a thousand heartrending disabilities. Blind girls no longer walk Main Street, wielding pointers like champion épéeists; blind boys no longer turn full Nelsons on befuddled sighted kids who are left to gasp, "How the hell did he do that?" The school has once more retreated unto itself; it employs about 200 locals, many performing such saintly duties as the changing of diapers and the pushing of wheelchairs. But the 75 students are again out of sight (ours as well as theirs) if not always mind.

Will we let the wonderful metaphor of the Blind School fade to black just like that? No! For the campus, but two blocks from the Kauffman homestead, has been ancestral ground since the 1920s, when my Irish grandmother signed on as a teacher of braille. The surrounding landscape is mine, by spiritual if not contractual inheritance: I see it daily, in light and in dreams. The school is flanked by chestnut trees and fronted by a row of towering maples. Across the street is Centennial Park, a gently sloping host of oak trees, an eerily autumnal grove through which I like to imagine Ichabod Crane galloping in full October panic. Through leafless boughs I worship its Halloween moon with pagan ardency.

In autumn, Lucine and Gretel and I gather chestnuts from the trees on the campus of the Blind School, just as my brother, Mike, and I did as boys, and as our father did before us. We dodge acorns shaken from the oak by frantic squirrels, who are resentful of the competition from bipeds who don't even eat the damned nuts we pick. On Sundays we sit under a spreading chestnut tree reading aloud poems about September by Bliss Carman and Helen Hunt Jackson, verse that invariably rhymes "goldenrod" with "God." We throw acorns at cavities in the trees, with about as much success as when I toss a basketball at the undersized hoop along a carnival midway.

Two million miles and one television set away from your night-mare, urban man, I pitch a blue-and-white foam UB Bulls football to Gretel, who eludes Lucine and sprints over the sward of chestnut leaves to a touchdown. Washington, Manhattan, Kabul, Baghdad, Jerusalem, Los Angeles: I haven't the slightest desire to interfere with your worlds. Why won't you vouchsafe the same benign neglect to mine?

I have passed the Blind School so many thousands of times that I am every bit as sightless as its most afflicted student—except in those random moments of heightened sentience, when God's face is writ in every maple leaf, every scurrying squirrel, every chest-nut husk.

Under a harvest moon we walk to Van Detta Stadium, cutting across the Blind School along the beaten path that Dad told me was an "old Indian trail." I repeat this wholesome fib to Gretel. I tread in my own boyish footsteps, imprinted as a teenager on crisp fall nights when I nursed absurd fantasies about being asked to the Sadie Hawkins Dance by a real live girl (fat chance!).

On fall Friday nights I sit in the rickety visitors' bleachers at Van Detta Stadium, watching the Batavia Blue Devils football team. I am surrounded by wizened Italians and embittered ex-jocks who curse the coach's play-calling, the referee's sight—and woe betide the black quarterback who messes up. But let the spectator's third cousin make a block on a five-yard punt return and it's whooping and hol-lering and "Waytago, Jimmy!" and high-fives all around. Buying a styrofoam cup of hot chocolate from the Lions Club stand at halftime, I see the older boys who walked as giants when I was young: the quarterback who went away to college and came back a lawyer and is resented still (consistent with the timeless working-class suspicion of Cornell); the potbellied jocks (I should talk!) replaying olden touchdowns in an alcoholic fugue; the forty-five-year-old ex-waterboy, still deferential around the gridiron gods. This is my Sep-tember, "dearest month of all to pensive minds," as the lugubrious

New England poet Carlos Wilcox held, and its pellucidity is thrown into sharpest focus by my beloved Blind School.

My one and only play, commissioned by the Genesee County Bicentennial Committee, was written to be performed at the Blind School upon the county's 200th birthday. I titled it *Joseph Ellicott and His Amazing Technicolor Dream,* very hiply associating myself with a Donny Osmond vehicle.

A farrago of Genesee-centric witticisms and groan-inducing puns, the play—or "your little skit," as one of Batavia's innumerable eccentric old ladies called it—could not be called Pinteresque. I squeezed every comic possibility out of Batavia founder Joseph Ellicott's suicide, and placed front and center such literary Geneseeans as John Gardner and John Yates, willfully misleading my neighbors into the conceit that ours is a county enveloping many men of letters.

As acutely sensitive to social issues as the most jerk-kneed Stanley Kramer film, I jammed in a pro-Italian scene with all the delicacy of a fisting sailor. I nixed a suggested Parade of Happy Immigrants, and I left Ellicott's boss, the Italo-Dutch banker Paolo Busti, in his locker—I didn't have the right token to open it. In Busti's stead I featured an Italian immigrant named Virgilio Ranzoni, who in the 1920s sought to organize the gypsum mines of nearby Oakfield for far and away my favorite union, the anarchistic Wobblies, who sang songs of the sabby-cat and took no shit from bosses or urban commies.

With such arrant agit-prop dropped into the minefield of broad jokes, the play bid fair to become the most powerful piece of social commentary since the Monkees' "Pleasant Valley Sunday." Sockdolager, old boy! Sockdolager!

Yet here I must dispense with the false modesty and self-deprecation. The play was a smash. We shattered the box office record at the Genesee Community College theater, to which *Joseph Ellicott* was moved by the inventive director Peggy Marone. On opening night, we had to turn people away. A capacity crowd of 325 neighbors laughed, cheered, and howled as a terrific cast, led by St. Joe's business manager, John McGee, as the comically choleric Ellicott, brought our ancestors to life. The Italian miner was beautifully played by attorney Michael Del Plato, cousin of Mad Vinny the muralist. In the play's emotional centerpiece, he put grande dame Mary Richmond in her place. Mary was played by Lucine, who had intended to try out for the part of Madam Edna. A snob or a whore: a dramatic stretch in either case, I assure you. And in a symbolic burying of the muck hoe, if not the hatchet, Carol Grasso, the anti-Muckdog, got the biggest laugh of the night with the punch line "mothermucker." I walked away from that play as proud as I have ever been in my life.

Even here, I walked in the steps of my forefathers. For there once was a (part-time) Geneseean who had a hit play on Broadway, and a frothy piece of radicalism it was.

George S. Brooks, a dear friend of Henry W. Clune, was a farm boy from Wyoming County's Pearl Creek. (Pronounced "crick," though I suspect that the adult George, who signed on with the Manhattan martini-bantering team, used the long double *e*.) George spent a brief time in Batavia as a newspaperman with the *Daily News*, but our burg wasn't big enough to hold the expansive and burbling Brooks, who by the 1930s was the most consistent manufacturer of short stories (mostly about football or fraternity hijinks) for *The Saturday Evening Post*.

Spread Eagle (1927), the play Brooks wrote with Walter B. Lister, is a change of pace on the order of Jean Genet writing Bible stories for children. A satire of U.S. gunboat diplomacy in Mexico, *Spread Eagle* is a fast-moving and pointed send-up of American imperialism that time has not dulled. Brooks was the former commander of the Tompkins County American Legion Post, but then Middle America was once solidly anti-imperialist, while the coasts—or at least Gotham City and Babylon West—mongered war. (Brooks's buddy Henry W. Clune was a bourgeois Republican who publicly opposed

U.S. involvement in World Wars I and II, Korea, Vietnam, and Iraq—a pacifist quintet.)

In the late 1990s, director James Glossman and the gruffly lovable old socialist Ed Asner discovered *Spread Eagle* quite by accident. They persuaded the Los Angeles Theater Works to record an audio-tape version of the play featuring a veritable *Love Boat*-ful of washed-up television players, including Fred "Wonder Years" Savage and Sharon "Cagney and Lacey" Gless.

For years I had urged *Spread Eagle* upon the local greasepaint and stagelights crowd, to no effect—but now I had Ed Asner in my quiver: Mr. Graaaant! himself. George S., the forgotten yokel, the dramaturge of our sublunary region, had just had his ticket validated in the empyrean!

I contacted star and director. Mr. Asner was as gracious as could be; Mr. Glossman was effusive in his praise of Brooks's "lost American classic" and desirous of staging a production in the hinterlands, with an eye toward Broadway. The cast loved the play, he said, and would hop on the first plane to Rochester should the artistic director of the Flower City's largest theater company beckon. Giddy with the possibilities—our Mr. Brooks the talk of the town, his play revived before packed western New York audiences as real live TV stars recited his witty badinage—I contacted the panjandrums of Rochester theater. I was a veritable impresario: "Here you are, fellows; let me drop *this* hit in your lap! A famous cast performing a sparkling play by a forgotten playwright from your own backyard!" What could be better?

Oh, Bill. Foolish lad. Why do you always forget in the adrenalin rush that you live in the provinces and that the stewards of provincial culture despise nothing so much as a homegrown artist? The ministers of art could not have been less interested, unless perhaps I had proposed an adaptation of a John Gardner work. So George S. Brooks remains obscure, and at odd moments I fume over what might have been.

Before World War II, when book-length poems were actually published without NEA subvention and bought by people who intended
to read them and often did, Josephine Young Case, the daughter of
electro-mogul Owen D. Young of General Electric, wrote *At Midnight
on the 31st of March*. In her fantasy, a small Upstate town awakes to
find that it has been cut off from the rest of the world—if, indeed,
the rest of the world even exists anymore. After an initial period of
bewilderment, Mrs. Case's townfolk of Saugersville survive by dint
of cooperative effort, native ingenuity, and the use of those resources
indigenous to the area. The older ones begin to remember:

> *When Saugersville set fashions for itself,*
> *I mean to say we had our own ways here*
> *That weren't like the ways of Centerfield or Steck,*
> *Much less the ways of any city place*
> *Where most of us had never been at all.*

After a year of isolation, "they knew each other as they never
had"; they come to realize:

> *The life is harder than it used to be,*
> *But troubles are more real. We're thankful that*
> *What's bad, or good, is right beneath your hand,*
> *You know just where you're at, and what to do.*
> *We're all of us more real, and more alive,*
> *And Saugersville is real, more like a town,*
> *And not a gas-pump on a concrete road.*

All of us more real. How about it? You may say that I'm a dreamer,
but I'm not the only one. Michael Eisner is not my King, Madonna
is not my Queen. We are a globe of villages, not a global village.
One John Hodgins painting of the Tonawanda Creek is worth a thousand downloaded images from the (Bill) Gates of Hell. Ruth McEvoy,
in writing her history of our town, is satisfied in a way that Elizabeth

Dole never can be, no matter how many boner pills her impotent husband pops. The father who might drink a bit too much beer and curse a blue streak but who walks his son through town, pointing out where the Tracys lived, where they used to play football in the autumn twilight, where Jack the Indian used to hunker down for the night to sleep it off, is living "family values" in a way that the epicene preachers of the Family Channel Right cannot dream of, even if they say "gee whillikers" and drink grape Nehi.

As a congenital optimist, I find signs of health, of life-enriching parochialism, even in as dispirited and beaten-down a town as Batavia. We endure, despite the mistakes and greed and pettiness, and we endure because, to my mind, a life lived locally is invested with a meaning that no tyrant, whether corporate or governmental, can take away. The colors have not been washed out of our flag yet.

Speak for the small, the stay-at-home, the front porch, and sooner or later you will be maligned as a Norman Rockwellite. Given Rockwell's swelling reputation, perhaps the knife is dulling. But still, the accusation carries the imputation of willful unreality. Hey: where are the unwed Hispanic mothers in your portrait, huh, Normie? Well?

In *Freedom from Want*, Rockwell's iconographic representation of Thanksgiving, our loveliest secular holiday, the aproned grandmother makes a reverential presentation of a stuffed turkey to a tableful of grinning menfolk and beaming gals. Oddly, no one in the painting is looking at Grandma; the progeny are making merry conversation and Grandpa is ravenously eyeing the bird, which in death has become rather more succulent than Grandma.

How would this scene play in today's America? Our twenty-first century Rockwell might well depict the children gazing in slack-jawed wonderment at the bearer of the turkey, as if to ask: "Who the hell is the old lady?"

Never before have there been so many grandparents in America, and yet, in a heartbreakingly large number of cases the job of grandparent has been reduced to sending Hallmark cards and gift-wrapped Disney videos to faraway grandchildren come Christmas. (Or, as the

tykes learn to call it in public school, the Holiday Season.) At
Thanksgiving, if the far-flung pilgrims of modern America do return,
they reconstitute the family like those reverse-action shots in movies,
in which an alien who has been blown to bits is made whole again.

These gatherings, however bathed in love, are marred by the
knowledge of their transience. They are glancing, evanescent, incom-
plete. The hugs and kisses and laughter that fill the TV time-outs
during the Lions game are pregnant with loss. For family life must
be continuous to have meaning; without proximity, kinship fades.
And today's families have everything but proximity.

I am blessed that almost every blood relative, near and distant,
lives within thirty miles of Batavia. We see each other all the time,
so that when we sit down to turkey and Grandma Baker's hand-
ground stuffing and Mom's pumpkin pie (which we are careful not to
praise too lavishly, lest Grandma take a burn), the holiday does not
resemble the all-too-common American experience: a table of tense
strangers or inwardly weeping mothers, dreading the weekend's good-
byes and tearful departures even before the grandkids (how they've
grown!) have carved out the first mashed-potato lakes.

The families of vagabonds seem to have selected Thanksgiving as
the time for the designated annual reunion, probably because it still
falls on a Thursday, and even the most Scrooge-ish nonretail employers have given up on squeezing any productivity out of the following
Friday. Thanksgiving was exempted from the shameful Uniform Holiday Act of 1968, under which Congress and LBJ, prodded by the
(progressive!) Chamber of Commerce and the travel industry, booted
holidays from their traditional dates and into the nearest Monday.
(The father of the three-day weekend, Florida Senator George Smath-
ers, best known as JFK's procurer, wanted to move Thanksgiving and
the Fourth of July to Monday as well. But not even the maudlin Texas
cracker in the White House was that far gone.)

Lest we forget, the hosts of the first Thanksgiving were not locals.
But our contemporary rootlessness is not so much in our genes as in

our policies. The domestic diaspora of the past sixty years is due more to government actions than to an invisible hand sending us hither and yon. Consider World War II, for which Rockwell's *Freedom from Want* sold war bonds. More than 15 million Americans, or 12 percent of the civilian population, resided in a different county in March 1945 than they had on December 7, 1941—and this doesn't even count the 12 million soldiers.

The dislocations of World War II and the Cold War, accelerated by the Interstate Highway System and federal subsidies to colleges and universities, led to a situation today in which one of every three Americans lives outside his natal state. In twelve states, natives are a minority of the population, most fantastically in Nevada, Bugsy Siegel's paradise, where 80 percent were born elsewhere. Nevada isn't a state: it's a hotel with senators.

At the opposite pole stands Pennsylvania, four-fifths of whose residents are homegrown. Thus the pop standard of American mobility, "Home for the Holidays," gets it all wrong with its line: "I met a man who lived in Tennessee and he was heading for/Pennsylvania and some homemade pumpkin pie." Keystone boys don't move.

"Mobility is associated with psychiatric casualty rates among both adults and children," wrote two researchers at Walter Reed who studied the emotional imbalances of peripatetic military brats. But don't hold your breath waiting for mobility to become a political issue. For what is Washington, D.C., if not one vast homeless center, sheltering the lawyers and student council presidents of Everywhere, U.S.A.?

Mobility is the great sickness crippling America, withering its civic life and deadening its spirit. But it remains undiagnosed, its symptoms mis-ascribed, for only the mobile have microphones and cameras and printer's ink. You never hear about the millions of stay-at-home Americans; we play the unheard music.

Before President Bush II's speechwriters declared a secular jihad to "rid the world of evil," restoring "civil society" was all the rage in white Washington. "Civil society" was on the lying lips of every rootless talking head and think-tank commander in the imperial city. But civil society is precisely what they and the empire they serve have sought to destroy. Civil society is Miss McEvoy publishing her history of Batavia; Mike Sheehan the Lecturing Knight setting up the Gennys at the Elks Club; Bud Brasky's Globetrotters sweating out the summer on the asphalt courts at Williams Park; a drunken Mason spitting on Captain Morgan's cenotaph; Catherine Roth, scourge of rodents, killing gophers in the Batavia Cemetery; Pastor Marty refusing to paint a bra on the mermaid; Steve Carr holding out for a few months more because, after all, it's his name on the store, and how will he break the news to Marilyn in Children's Wear?; and in my own anemic if well-meaning way, it is watching the Muckdogs and reading Gardner aloud and donating scripts about our ecclesiastical stained-glass windows and local architecture and the county's 200th birthday (worrying all the time that my jokes about "mothermuckers" might offend the great ladies of Batavia).

I remember profaning the sabbath a couple of years ago by watching a Sunday morning politics show. The repulsive civil society charlatan Bill Bennett was holding forth on television, the true and only milieu of his kind. How happily I clicked off his scowly jowls. For it was a glorious October morn, so I walked with Lucine and Gretel though the Blind School park. Gretel collected chestnuts from the trees that Progress has not seen fit to cut down as yet, the trees that supplied me and my brother with brown shopping-bagsful of these quite useless and altogether beautiful nuts. That Gretel may do the same with her children sustains me. For as the great-grandmother tells the boy in Ray Bradbury's *Dandelion Wine*, "No person ever died that had a family."

Seasons pass; I stay.

I have a *Daily News* of July 15, 1967, with a back page commemorating the opening of the MacArthur Park Community Pool and the adjacent wading pool. I am in two photos. In one, I am playing beachball catch with my brother as Jimmy Ambrose, who would die of cancer at a tragically young age, looks on. The caption reads "DON'T

DROP IT—Youngsters have a 'ball' in new wading pool." In the other, I am squinting into the camera with future Muckdogs president Dennis Dwyer and a Dwyer girl (there were so many of them; they were such good Irish-Catholics) over the caption, "HAPPY FACES—Small fry are all smiles as they rest on edge of pool."

The deep pool, which for its entire life would be known as the "new pool," closed a decade or so ago. There was a crack in the foundation, and the city fathers saw no reason to fix it. Who cares about foundations? The new pool was filled in and blacktopped and surmounted by basketball hoops that no one ever uses.

The wading pool is still filled every summer, though, and in the haze of July and memory I bring Gretel almost weekly. We dodge the floating Band-Aids disadhered from the skinned knees and scraped elbows of the Dakotas and Sierras and Chances.

Batavia changes; my Batavia endures. The heedless beget the heedless. Mansions, trees, churches—all fall down. That's just the way it is.

More and more I find comfort in cemeteries, especially the ancient ones. (Ancient by American standards, which are the only standards I know.)

Through the necropolis I stumble, half-drunk on Genesee, birdsong filling my ears, on a favonian April afternoon, looking for a new family plot. Lucine and I were not married in the church, despite my casual promise to Monsignor Schwartz that we would have our marriage blessed sometime, someplace. A casual promise, casually broken. So I cannot lie in consecrated ground near the mafiosi. My sacred ground will be next door, in the old Batavia Cemetery, hailing distance from my family, amid Masons and Anti-Masons, attar of pizza from Uncle Tony's flavoring the boneyard air. Home, sweet home.

I have inherited from my parents and both grandfathers their almost pathological hatred of traveling outside Genesee County. What is travel, after all, except substituting a series of meaningless encounters with strangers for the solidity, the solidarity, of home? "I am not much an advocate for traveling," wrote Emerson, "and I observe that men run away to other countries because they are not good in their own, and run back to their own because they pass for nothing in their new places. For the most part, only the light characters travel. Who are you that have no task to keep you at home?" asked Ralph just before setting out on his latest lecture tour. Where's Waldo, indeed? But the hypocrisy of my beloved Transcendentalists need not trouble us, and besides, Emerson's handyman Henry David stood on what he stood for.

"New England is quite as large a lump of earth as my heart can really take in," said Hawthorne. His heart was far more capacious than mine. Genesee County, and perhaps a bit of Wyoming and Orleans counties as well, is all my heart can take.

I suppose it bespeaks my constricted, costive imagination, my utter failure in the dreamworld of exotica, but I fear death because the afterworld may remove me from Batavia. I cannot conceive of a heaven that is preferable to my town; no angels more companionable than my family or friends; no celestial vistas more pleasing to my eye than the wrought-iron gates of the old Batavia Cemetery, the twilight-shadowed outfield fence at Dwyer, the scarlet and orange maples that overhang Hart Street in October. Oh Lord, if it's all the same with you, I'd just as soon stay here. Batavia needs its ghosts.

Acknowledgments

How do I begin to list, let alone thank, all those who helped me write this book? They live on every street and rest in every cemetery of Genesee County. My gratitude flows to each of them.

I am indebted to my ancestors for settling in Batavia and its environs, to my parents and grandparents for staying put, and to my wife and daughter for their love, good humor, and disinclination toward geographic (and upward) mobility.

Several folks provided aid and often comfort along the way. Thanks to Marge Cervone, Peter Mumford, Mike Ward, Peter Dzwonkoski, Peter H. Clune, Alan Crawford, Ed Flynn, Susan Conklin and the staff of the Genesee County History Department (Gale Conn-Wright, Lenore Abrams, Ellen Bachorski), and Paula Meyer, Dorothy Coughlin, and the ever-patient and wonderful ladies of the Richmond Memorial Library.

I'm grateful to the following editors, who allowed me to try out regional themes in their pages: Joseph Epstein, Karl Zinsmeister, Tom Fleming, Scott Richert, Kenneth Turan, Bill Bradford, and Erich Eichman.

The late Clyde Taylor, my agent, died a couple of days after selling the proposal for this book to Tom Bissell at Holt. Their faith emboldened me. I appreciate the services of Kirsten Manges, Clyde's protégée.

George Hodgman, my editor, made this book better. Less Masonic, perhaps, but better. I owe him a motorcyle ride.

Finally, a long overdue thanks to Carlos (wherever you are), Karl, Hugo, and Bob, who once upon a time got me thinking. . . .

Excerpt from *Upstate* by Edmund Wilson. Copyright © 1971 by Edmund Wilson. Copyright renewed 2000 by Helen Miranda Wilson. Reprinted by permission of Farrar, Straus and Giroux, LLC.

Excerpt from *Remembering* by Wendell Berry. Copyright © 1988 by Wendell Berry. Reprinted by permission of North Point Press, a division of Farrar, Straus and Giroux, LLC.

Lyrics from "New York Country Song" by Todd Hobin. Copyright © 1978 by Todd Hobin Music BMI. Reprinted by kind permission of Todd Hobin.

Lyrics from "Passion Is No Ordinary Word" by Graham Parker. Reprinted by kind permission of Graham Parker.

"The Lesson" from *My Kind of Country* by Carl Carmer (Syracuse University Press, Syracuse, N.Y., 1995). By permission of the publisher.

Excerpt from *I Always Liked it Here* by Henry W. Clune. By kind permission of Peter H. Clune.

Excerpt from *Existential Errands*. Copyright © 1972 by Norman Mailer. Reprinted with the permission of The Wylie Agency, Inc.

Excerpt from *The Bit Between My Teeth* by Edmund Wilson. Copyright © 1965, renewed 1993 by Helen Miranda Wilson. Reprinted by permission of Farrar, Straus and Giroux, LLC.

The Resurrection, by John Gardner. Copyright © 1966 by John Gardner. Reprinted by permission of Georges Borchardt, Inc.

Nickel Mountain, by John Gardner. Copyright © 1963, 1966, 1971, 1972, 1973 by John Gardner. Reprinted by permission of Georges Borchardt, Inc.

On Moral Fiction, by John Gardner. Copyright © 1978 by John Gardner. Reprinted by permission of Georges Borchardt, Inc.

"Redemption," from *The Art of Living and Other Stories*, by John Gardner. Copyright © 1981 by John Gardner. Reprinted by permission of Georges Borchardt, Inc.

Stillness by John Gardner. Copyright © 1986 by The Estate of John Gardner. Reprinted by permission of Georges Borchardt, Inc.

Freddy's Book, by John Gardner. Copyright © 1980 by John Gardner. Reprinted by permission of Georges Borchardt, Inc.

Mickelsson's Ghosts, by John Gardner. Copyright © 1982 by John Gardner. Reprinted by permission of Georges Borchardt, Inc.

Excerpts from *At Midnight on the Thirty-First of March* by Josephine Young Case. Copyright 1938 by Josephine Young Case; copyright © renewed 1966 by Josephine Young Case. Reprinted by permission of Houghton Mifflin Company. All rights reserved.

Lyrics from "(There's No Place Like) Home for the Holidays," reprinted with permission of Charlie Deitcher Productions.

About the Author

Bill Kauffman is the author of *Every Man a King*; *Country Towns of New York*; *With Good Intentions?: Reflections on the Myth of Progress in America*; and *America First! Its History, Culture, and Politics.* He writes often for *The Independent* in London, *The Wall Street Journal*, and *The American Enterprise.* Although Batavia remains first in his heart, he currently resides five miles away in Elba, New York, with his wife, Lucine, and daughter, Gretel.